Tombstone's
Treasure

TOMBSTONE's *Treasure*

SILVER MINES AND GOLDEN SALOONS

Sherry Monahan

FOREWORD BY BOB BOZE BELL

UNIVERSITY OF NEW MEXICO PRESS
ALBUQUERQUE

YEAR   PRINTING
12 11 10 09 08 07   1 2 3 4 5 6

Library of Congress Cataloging-in-Publication Data

Monahan, Sherry A.
    Tombstone's treasure : silver mines and golden saloons / Sherry
Monahan / foreword by Bob Boze Bell.
        p. cm.
    Includes bibliographical references and index.
    ISBN 978-0-8263-4176-1 (pbk. : alk. paper)
    1. Tombstone (Ariz.)—History. 2. Frontier and pioneer life—
Arizona—Tombstone. 3. Tombstone (Ariz.)—Social life and customs.
4. Bars (Drinking establishments)—Arizona—Tombstone—History.
5. Silver mines and mining—Arizona—Tombstone—History.
6. Amusements—Arizona—Tombstone—History. I. Title.
    F819.T6M66 2007
    979.1'53—dc22
                                2006037835

Book design and composition by Damien Shay
Body type is Utopia 9.5/13
Display is Aachen and Bickley Script

For my dad,

John Philip Teeter

May he be looking
down from heaven
with a proud smile.

Contents

List of Illustrations

LIST OF ILLUSTRATIONS

Guys like me are obsessed with thirty seconds in the history of America's most legendary boom town. That's a pretty narrow window for any town to be judged, but that's what it has come down to for Tombstone and the gunfight near the O.K. Corral.

But, after the arguing and petty bickering over what color hatband Tom McLaury wore (it was silver) and whether Wyatt Earp wore a holster during the thirty-second gunfight (he didn't; he put his pistol in his coat pocket), some of us Earp and cowboy fanatics want to know what kind of town the most famous gunfight in the West took place in. That's where a book like this shines like a beacon in the darkest night.

It is both shocking and enlightening to learn just how sophisticated Tombstone really was when the Earps, Doc Holliday, Johnny Ringo, and Curly Bill strode the boardwalks. Tombstone actually had telephones, ice cream parlors, coffee shops, a bowling alley, and a swimming pool. Wow! It is so contrary to the Hollywood version of the town—it reads like science fiction, but it's absolutely true.

It should come as no surprise that Tombstone had these things and more simply because of the wealth that the mines generated. One mining company alone, in 1881, produced over $433,000 worth of bullion in eight months! Once the money was made, the men in town dropped their dividends at the elegant saloons, dance houses, and played high-stake faro, monte, and other gaming tables. Sherry Monahan has brought to life the West's most infamous town and given us a great insight into the way it really was. What a town! What a book! Thanks Sherry, for a job well done.

Preface

M y love of Tombstone and the old West has led me down the "Town Too Tough to Die" path yet again. So many people are aware of Tombstone's existence due to one thirty-second gunfight that took place on October 26, 1881. Wyatt Earp, his brothers, and John "Doc" Holliday would never have even been in Tombstone if it weren't for two things—silver mines and saloons. Tombstone was teeming with money because of the mining, and the saloons benefited heavily from that wealth. With high-priced fancy cocktails, monte, faro, and poker, saloons were very profitable businesses.

This was no ordinary desert town—it was, as Val Kilmer (portraying Doc Holliday in *Tombstone*) said, "Very cosmopolitan." It's my continuing love affair with this town that has inspired me to write yet another book about its exciting history.

I hope that you, too, find Tombstone's past as exciting as I do.

Introduction

While it's true that the street fight between the Earps and Doc Holliday and the Clantons and McLaurys behind the O.K. Corral often overshadows the history of Tombstone, Arizona, the town itself was prosperous and quite wealthy because of its productive silver mines.

Once rich mineral deposits were discovered in Tombstone, its population swelled and so did its wealth. Tombstone's boom lasted longer than most mining towns' did, and Tombstone eventually became "family oriented," as residents became confident in their future. Tombstone was a wealthy mining community during the 1880s and was often compared to San Francisco when it came to sophistication. There were fraternal organizations, churches, numerous social events, upscale hotels, and elegant saloons.

This mining boomtown sat atop one of the most productive mining areas in the Southwest. Tombstone's mines peaked from mid-1879 to late 1883, and during this pinnacle, the mines produced, on average, over five million dollars annually in silver and gold. The larger mining companies paid an average of six hundred thousand dollars in dividends annually.

In addition to the breweries, wine rooms, saloons, and dance houses, there were other types of entertainment available for hardworking men. The sources of entertainment covered the spectrum from sophisticated theater programs to rough and rowdy cockfights, and everything in between. Tombstone boasted a racetrack, bowling alley, skating rink, baseball games, boxing matches, and more, which kept many a resident entertained in the most lively silver mining camp Arizona has ever seen. Tombstone's number of saloons reflected the town's boom. When it first "hit" in mid-1880, there were about twenty-six saloons and breweries. By July of the following year, the number of saloons in Tombstone had doubled. The year 1881 was no doubt the best year for Tombstone's saloons, and the quantity of them was never higher. By the end of 1882, the count of Tombstone's drinking houses had fallen back down to about thirty.

Tombstone saloonkeepers entertained their customers with classical music, or tunes played by Tombstone's brass band, or an Italian string ensemble. Even though these saloons were more or less respectable, Tombstone's society women did not go into them because no respectable woman dared enter a saloon—it was just not proper. Not to mention that men did not want them there; this was a place where they could seek solace among their brethren. Alcohol and music aside, Tombstone's saloons drew crowds because of the gambling.

Gambling concessions and cigar stands were nestled in the saloons, and were often run by someone other than the saloon owners. Most had a separate section for gambling, usually in the back. However, the reader should not envision that old Hollywood image of a secluded, smoke-filled room where a bunch of desperadoes were ready to kill one another over a hand of cards. It is true a gambler could get shot over a game of cards, but only if he was caught cheating. The most popular saloon games of the time were faro, monte, and poker, but other saloons offered keno, roulette, and twenty-one.

Tombstone's glory days lasted until about 1887, even though mining had all but ceased in 1886. Hopeful investors tried to mine Tombstone once more in the 1890s and early 1900s, but their efforts eventually failed.

This book was written to share interesting true tales, reveal Tombstone's mining and gambling history, and allow readers to drift back into a different locale where wealthy businesspeople and rugged miners rubbed elbows at the bar and gambled side by side. Old newspapers, photographs, reference books, and dusty record books almost seem to come alive to tell their stories. They provide a glimpse of what the past was like and allow us to understand life from a different and exciting time.

Chapter One

Settin' Up Camp

Tombstone's Discovery
and Its Silver Mines

A fter Tombstone's founder, Ed Schieffelin, discovered silver in Tombstone's hills, people came by the thousands. The first to set up camp were hopeful miners and prospectors, followed by assayers, businessmen, and eventually their families.

Before all that though, Ed roamed Arizona Territory searching for silver and gold. Fearing Indians, he tagged along with an army scout team who eventually stopped at Fort Huachuca, some twenty miles from the rich Tombstone hills. Ed used "Camp Huachuca" as his home base while he made several prospecting trips to the Apache-filled hills. Upon his return, his army buddies often told him, "You'll find your tombstone if you don't stop running through this country all alone as you are, while the Indians are so bad."[1] That statement left an impression on the soon-to-be-very-rich Ed, and he named his first mine "Tombstone." Later, the town that blossomed to support the silver mining boom adopted the same name.

1877–78

Ed eventually located some very rich ore samples in those Indian-ridden hills in the summer and fall of 1877. Being out of provisions, and anxious for assayers to see his samples, Ed made his way to Tucson. He tried to show his ore samples to possible investors, but few looked at them, as they had no interest in mining. Those who did look said they were very low grade and not worth much. Ed soon

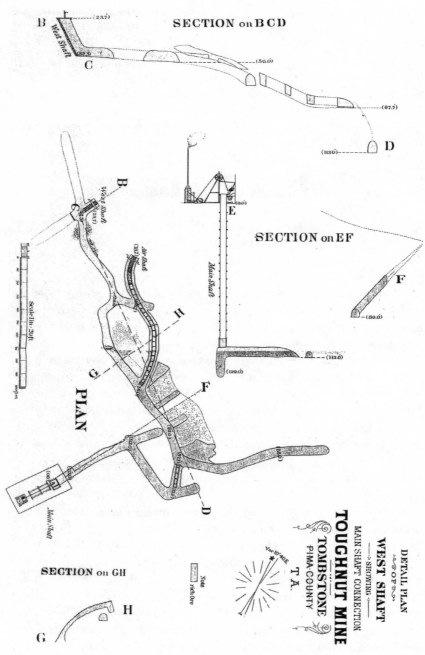

Toughnut mining map, 1880s, courtesy of the Arizona Historical Society.

realized Tucson would yield nothing, so he went in search of his brother, Al, who was also in the territory. After a long, hard search, Ed found his brother working at the McCracken mines.[2] He immediately showed the ore samples to Al. His brother responded like the naysayers in Tucson, saying the ore grade was very low. Since Ed was unable to have an actual assay made on the ore, he was unable to prove his confidence in the rock. With nowhere else to turn, Ed took a job where his brother worked, filling buckets at the mines. Luckily, Ed was working at the mine when Richard Gird, an assayer, paid a visit to the McCracken mines.

Ed, seeing an opportunity to have an assay made on his rocks, showed Gird the ore. Gird was immediately impressed with Ed's samples and said the value could range anywhere from forty to two thousand dollars per ton. Gird was so impressed with Ed's samples that the three men quickly left on February 14 to go back to the hills where Ed had found the ore. They arrived on February 26, 1878, and by March 15, had located the Lucky Cuss mine, and on March 22 the Toughnut mine.[3] A couple of prospectors, who had lost their mules, happened upon the Schieffelins and Richard Gird. Gird encouraged them to stay, saying the prospecting was good. After a couple of weeks they were ready to quit because they had discovered nothing, but Gird talked them into staying a little while longer. Lucky for Hank William and Jack Oliver, because shortly thereafter, they discovered one of Tombstone's best mines—the Grand Central.[4] One of the men was so happy at their discovery he went to Fort Huachuca to celebrate. He began to tell of his find, which excited quite a few listeners. White Parsons heard this story and traveled to the mining camp. Ed, Al, and Richard Gird sold their Contention mine to Parsons for ten thousand dollars.[5]

Once the Schieffelin party was convinced they had found something significant, they needed financing. As luck would have it, they had already met the man who would help them finance their vision when they passed through Tucson. His name was John S. Vosburg, and he was a business partner and personal friend of Governor Safford. When Ed and his group arrived in Tucson, they had been advised by the governor to see Vosburg. They arrived at Vosburg's business and upon entering, Gird said, "We would like to talk with you privately. The governor has told us to come to you, that you were close mouthed and discreet. Would you mind shutting the door?" Vosburg proceeded to shut and lock the door. Gird continued, "We are prospectors and have reason to think there may be something worth looking for in the

Chiricahua Mountains. We are on our way there but need more supplies. Can you help?"[6] Vosburg took them across the street to Lord & Williams's mercantile store and supplied them with three hundred dollars worth of goods. They soon departed for Tombstone, and Vosburg did not hear from them for a while. About ten days later, Gird appeared and told Vosburg that they had indeed found something "quite promising." They were in need of more supplies and black powder. Gird took back most of the necessary items, but had to wait for the powder, which Vosburg delivered himself.

Vosburg retold this story to Frank C. Lockwood in 1925. "An idea occurred to me. I knew nothing about prospecting and the governor not much more. If the trio have found something good and big they will need funds for developing. They know and trust the governor. The governor knows men with money." He then contacted the governor and advised him of his idea. The governor was sold. Since Vosburg had convinced the governor, he in turn convinced the Corbin brothers of the Corbin House Hardware Store in Connecticut to visit Tombstone. After visiting some of the mines, they, too, were convinced of the prospects. Vosburg, on behalf of himself and the governor, made an arrangement with the Schieffelin brothers and Gird to furnish enough money, not exceeding eighty thousand dollars, to build a ten-mill stamp and purchase all the necessary tools to crush the ore. For doing this, Vosburg and the governor retained a one-quarter interest in their mine holdings, including the Lucky Cuss, Toughnut, West Side, and Owl's Nest. While this was a good deal for Vosburg and the governor, they did not have eighty thousand dollars, so Vosburg made an agreement with the Corbin brothers of Connecticut to supply the eighty thousand dollars. In return for their loan, they received half of Vosburg and the governor's one-quarter interest in the mines.[7]

Once the flood of "sure enough" miners and their pack burros hit Tombstone, the mining exploded. Grand Central mine discoverers William and Oliver eventually sold out to the Grand Central Mining Company, which formed its organization on July 5, 1879. The company was incorporated in St. Louis, Missouri, and its president was W. H. H. Witherell. E. B. Gage, L. N. Thomas, and M. L. Gould were also officers with the company. One of their bylaw articles stated: "The objects for which said Company is formed are erecting, maintaining, and working stamping mills and furnaces, and all accompanying metallurgical appliances for the purpose of reducing Gold, Silver, Copper, and other metals and minerals, and refining same; for manufacturing such metals and minerals into the various useful and ornamental thereof, which are or may be the subject of commerce; for purchasing, leasing, and selling mines and mineral lands and lodes; for the purchase, lease, possession, and sale of land, or such interest or estate therein as may be necessary or convenient to effectuate any of the objects of said company; for repurchasing and selling metals and minerals and the various products thereof, and carrying on a general mining business, and for such other purposes as may be necessary to effectuate all the objects of said company."

Tombstone's hills proved Ed's army buddies wrong, and Tombstone's mining prospects were touted as the best ever discovered in the territory. Although the hills were promising, getting to them was not an easy task.

In 1878, the train only went as far as Yuma, and from there, fortune seekers rode stagecoaches, came by horseback, or drove wagons to Tucson. People traveling from San Francisco took the train by way of Casa Grande and the stage to Tucson. Those coming from the east would have come through St. Louis, Kansas City, and Las Vegas, New Mexico. The stage journey from Tucson was uphill and took about seventeen hours, but those leaving Tombstone only had to endure a twelve-hour return ride. Stagecoach journeys along this route were often hazardous, especially since the territory was filled with cattle thieves, ruffians, and hostile Apache Indians. The climate was also unpredictable along this seventy-two-mile journey, with the blazing hot sun shining during the day, and cool, windy nights.

Despite the many challenges, people came to Tombstone almost daily. By September 1878, when fortune-seekers first arrived they were dependent on storekeepers Amos W. Stowe and Cadwell & Stanford to keep them supplied with provisions. These stores were located at a small community known as Watervale, which was established to support the mines. Cadwell not only sold provisions at his store, but also carried passengers in a wagon he called Pioneer Tombstone Stage Lines. Technically, this was the first stage to operate in the Tombstone area, having started in the summer of 1878. Watervale was about three miles from the Tombstone mines and quickly proved inconvenient.

Two more towns were born from the mining industry. Richmond was started near the Lucky Cuss mine site, while the other was settled on one of the Toughnut Company's mines. The first Tombstone was on the site of the West Side mine, about one hundred yards southeast of the 1880 Fire House, in the fall of 1878. This location was on the hill across from present-day Tombstone. The West Side mine site prospered and, by the end of the year, boasted a saloon called Danner & Owens, Ike Clanton's Star Restaurant, and a post office.

1879

As 1879 was christened, the Tombstone Milling & Mining Company was established. Its officers were Anson P. K. Safford, president; D. C. Field, secretary; and Richard Gird, superintendent. The company's directors included Anson P. K. Safford, Richard Gird, Philip Corbin, and the Schieffelin brothers.

The Corbin brothers' involvement meant significant capital for the mining industry. They supplied the funds to build the mill needed for ore crushing, cleared an ore road from the mines to the mill, built a dam, and constructed a mile-and-one-eighth ditch and flume, which carried water to the mills and also provided power to the mill. By early summer, the first stamp dropped on Tombstone's precious silver ore, mined from the Toughnut. John Vosburg, who was involved from the beginning, recounted the day when the mill was first turned on. He said, "Turn on the water. It is a fine bright day. The water springs hurriedly at the wheel, the shafts turn on, the wheels go round, the rock-breaker opens its hungry jaws, some ore is fed to it, and the mill starts on its initial run of two months without stopping once. Gird has built a fine mill, and it runs beautifully, withal making lots of noise, which was lovely music."[8]

During the next five anxious days, Vosburg said the ore was fed into and broken by the rock breaker. It then fell into the batteries and was pounded through a forty screen mesh (forty meshes to the inch). It was then passed into pans and blended with quicksilver to be ground even finer. It was then sent to the "settler" where the amalgam or mixture became thick enough to be taken out and put in the retort. The retort, with heat, volatized the quicksilver, which was saved, and the residue was turned into bullion. Vosburg said

> While boss is melting the bullion and pouring the bar, I wish
> to say the aforementioned five days seemed to drag slowly
> by. We awoke frequently at night to listen to the lullaby of
> the stamps and never grumbled once—and then sleep again
> with golden dreams. Our most welcome first bar of bullion
> was tested carefully but hurry-upedlly [*sic*] and pronounced
> worth, with silver at 98 cents, $1,864 and some cents. We

shook hands all around and sang something appropriate—
let us hope.[9]

Before March 1879, many realized the need for yet another site for
their camp to grow. The West Side mine site, just under ten acres, was
too small. This decision may have also been forced after a windstorm
leveled the site in February. On March 5, a town site association was
established by Governor Anson P. K. Safford, Judge Thomas J. Bidwell,
A. J. Palmer, J. S. Clark, and C. H. Calhoun, who laid out a 320-acre
town site, where present-day Tombstone sits. The new camp evolving
in the district was officially called Tombstone, after Ed's old Army buddies' parting words. Judge Bidwell was originally in charge of the association, but in June, Michael Gray bought C. H. Calhoun's interest and
was put in charge.

Hearing of Tombstone's rich mines, Surveyor-General John W.
Wasson paid a visit to Tombstone's mining district. Despite his reputation as being a "bear" in mining matters, Wasson spoke highly of the
Tombstone district. He stated, "Tombstone mines have never been as
highly represented as their actual merits plainly justify, and . . . the
owners of leading claims there have been absolutely modest in speak-
ing of them."[10] Wasson also noted miners made more cuts, deepened
their tunnels, and removed ore samples to ascertain the value of the
mines on a daily basis. While the values were not for public knowledge, many knew the sample values averaged hundreds, and frequently reached thousands, of dollars.

It wasn't until early summer, however, that buildings began to go
up on the new site, according to an old Tombstone pioneer named
William N. Miller.[11] Miller stated that when he arrived in Tombstone in
May, there were no houses on the current Tombstone site. By August
though, Tombstone had begun to blossom. Miller recalled Charley
Brown's Hotel as first being made of canvas, ocotillo, and bear grass.
He described it as a saloon and boarding house combined, principally
to board the miners working at the Toughnut mine. Tombstone's
streets were gradually cleared from the corner of Third and Allen. After
supper most nights, some of the miners cleared areas for the streets
until four main roads ran into camp. Miller recalled, "Brown's place
was started as a boarding place for miners working on the Toughnut
and surrounding mines and was a man's town, known as Stagtown.
Families lived in Old Town, Richmond, and Watervale. There were no
women in Stagtown through July, except 'Birds of Passage.'"[12]

Miners worked both night and day shifts on three of Tombstone's most advanced mines—the Lucky Cuss, Contention, and Toughnut. The Toughnut, however, was already so well developed that the ore lay in piles, waiting to be crushed at the stamp mill. The Toughnut and the Lucky Cuss also had numerous cuts, tunnels, and shafts ranging from a few feet to 75 feet. The Contention had two shafts, one at 130 feet and the other at 110 feet, a 250-foot tunnel, and some crosscuts at the 110-foot level.

The walls in Tombstone's mines were made of porphyry and limestone, which necessitated drilling and blasting.[13] The drilling was done by hand and dynamite was used as the explosive. Few of the mines needed timber supports inside them, and water had not yet surfaced. Ore was hoisted from the mines by using a windlass on all the shafts except for the main one.[14] Once all the ore was hoisted to the main shaft, it was placed in kibbles, where a twenty-horsepower engine raised it to the surface.[15] Once aboveground, the ore was dumped into wheelbarrows. Two tramways with windlasses assisted the transportation of the kibbles on the incline in a shaft. Dumping platforms were located near the windlasses from which the ore was shoveled into the ore wagons for shipment to the mill. It cost $4.15 per ton to haul the ore over good roads to the mill with fifteen tons to a team of sixteen mules. It cost the company eight dollars to mine a ton of ore, $4.15 to haul it, and $6.00 to reduce a ton of ore at the mill, for a total of $18.15 to "work" a ton of pay ore.[16]

The miners at the Tombstone Milling & Mining Company worked in two shifts of ten hours per day. Stearine candles were used for underground illumination. Ventilation was "natural" in the company's shafts, because they were connected to the air and main shafts.[17] The miners were paid four dollars per day, laborers earned three dollars per day, and mechanics, carpenters, and bricklayers earned five to seven dollars per day.

Many businesses appeared in tents along the main streets of Tombstone. There were hotels, meat markets, bakeries, saloons, and a newspaper. On October 2, 1879, the *Nugget* printed its first edition under the journalistic talent of Artemus E. Fay in a building just east of Schieffelin Hall. The *Nugget* was quick in reporting its town's progress and said, "No mining camp on the Pacific coast ever started to build with the great promise that Tombstone does today." Promising it was; they even claimed Tombstone would be the Leadville of Arizona. The camp grew rapidly but was stalled for lack of available lumber. Thirty-four buildings were under contract, awaiting the arrival of supplies. Once the lumber was received, the tents were replaced with frame or adobe structures. These new buildings gave the appearance of a more "civilized" camp.

By August, pioneer Miller noted Stagtown had either "won out" or lost, depending upon how one looked at it.[18] Families began to arrive and settle in Tombstone, which grew by leaps and bounds.

Toward the end of the year, Tombstone was described as a town with pure air and unpolluted water. The climate was delightful, the days were warm, and the nights were cool. While the city appeared to have its water sources secure, lumber was still scarce. Any timber in Tombstone was brought in from the Dragoon or Huachuca Mountains, at a cost of fifty and sixty-five dollars per one thousand feet, respectively. Fortunately for Tombstone, adobe building material was abundant. Adobe, or sun-dried clay, was fairly durable when protected by a projecting roof to avoid washouts.

The end of 1879 was a significant period for Tombstone and its population of about one thousand. The village, by a vote of the people, became incorporated under the order of the county supervisors. Tombstone residents elected attorney William A. Harwood as their first official mayor, and they were on their way to becoming a stable community.

1880

Tombstone transformed from a tent-filled mining camp to a bustling community in 1880. Mining claims were staked daily, and the "boom" was underway. More people heard the positive statements about Tombstone, and it appeared everyone wanted a piece of the American pie. Tucson's *Arizona Daily Star* stated, "Tombstone is probably one of the most cosmopolitan camps this coast affords. Creed, color, and condition are not considered."[19]

Despite electing a mayor at the end of 1879, Tombstone held a new election in January 1880. Alder Randall was named mayor, while Sylvester Comstock, Harry Jones, Andrew Cadwell, and H. Smith were named city council members. Thomas J. Bidwell was also appointed justice of the peace and Michael Gray was appointed city clerk.

Two stagecoach companies continued delivering passengers to Tombstone, but by early 1880, H. C. Walker & Company became the Tucson & Tombstone Stage Line, run by William Ohnesorgen and Hiram Walker. John Kinnear still operated his stagecoach line, too.

Both companies ran stages between Tucson and Tombstone daily, each departing at 7:00 a.m. The Tucson & Tombstone Stage claimed its four-horse Concord coach made fast time, offered splendid meals along the way, traveled the best roads, and made the trip during daylight hours. Despite those claims, Kinnear's coaches continued to arrive first in Tombstone, mainly because they used a different route. Kinnear's coaches stopped at Ash Springs station where passengers were offered a "most interesting" dinner. Unfortunately, what they considered "most interesting" is unknown.

By February, hopeful mine stakers were disappointed when they arrived because there were no mines to be had. Even the "good prospects" were scarce, not to mention a rare find. Despite a lack of mining properties, many still came with picks and shovels in hand. The stages were crowded with women and children who had come to join their husbands and fathers. Because of these newcomers, Tombstone began building a school. Plans were also made to bring the railroad closer to Tombstone. Benson was the newest railroad town, named in honor of John Benson of San Francisco. For a while, this site was the main point from which Tombstone and southeastern freight was delivered.

As the building trade increased, the town's water supply decreased. The liquid was still trucked in from Watervale and Tombstone was desperate for its own water supply. Many complained that a large percentage of water was being consumed in the building trade, leaving citizens with little in which to bathe. As stagecoaches, wagon freighters, and ore wagons rolled down Tombstone's streets, dust flew horribly. Because of the dusty conditions, daily bathing was necessary, so with water in short supply and in great demand, the bathhouses increased their rates. Despite these inconveniences, Tombstone forged ahead. On April 22, 1880, the *Arizona Daily Star* even said the mines were "whooping-up."

Even though Tombstone's mines were just beginning to peak by the spring of 1880, Ed and Al Schieffelin decided to move on. Since Ed detested city life, he and Al capitalized on an opportunity to sell their mining interests. On March 15, 1880, they sold their entire interest to the Corbin brothers, Hamilton Disston of Philadelphia, and Marcus and Willis Hulings of Pennsylvania for six hundred thousand dollars. The money was paid in monthly installments, and the Schieffelins were still considered part of the company until the final payment was made. While the Schieffelin brothers were content to accept six hundred thousand dollars for their interests, their hold-ings were estimated to be worth two million dollars.[20] Richard Gird held his mining interest for about one year longer. Ed left Tombstone and headed for Nevada to prospect once more.

With the Schieffelin brothers gone, the Tombstone Milling & Mining Company reorganized. The new officers of the company were George Burnham, Philadelphia, president; Marcus Hulings, Oil City, Pennsylvania, first vice-president; Philip Corbin, New Britain, Connecticut, second vice-president; George S. Corbin, New York, New York, treasurer; Sylvester C. Dunham, Hartford, Connecticut, secre-tary; and Richard Gird, superintendent. Members of the board of directors included all the officers as well as Hamilton Disston, B. F. Hart, Willis J. Hulings, S. P. M. Tasker, and Charles T. Perry. Hamilton Disston and A. P. K. Safford later developed central Florida, including Tarpon Springs.

This company, made up of wealthy Eastern businessmen, included nine prosperous mines. Their holdings covered 180 acres of mineral ground and a mill site of five hundred acres along the San Pedro River, including the towns of Millville and Charleston. They also owned exclusive water rights to the Sonora line, which ran over twenty miles. Add to their already rich collection two mills, one ten-stamp wet crushing mill run by water power, and one fifteen-stamp dry crushing mill run by steam power. The value of the mines was seen in its ore production, and from June 1879 to March 14, 1880, one ten-stamp mill produced 148 bars, valued at over $316,124.94.[21]

Newspapers were an integral part of Tombstone's development. The *Nugget*, Tombstone's first, was now competing with the *Tombstone Epitaph*. Clum, Sorin & Co started the *Epitaph* on May 1, 1880. Both weekly papers carried mining news, local tidbits, and a wide variety of advertisements. The *Nugget* and the *Epitaph* also talked of expanding their news to daily papers. The *Arizona Quarterly Illustrated* maga-zine said, "If the town grows as it has in the past, and the prospects are fair that Tombstone will become an important point, as the mines attract population and capital to develop the wealth that lies waiting the prospector."

Tombstone's mines continued to produce quality bullion, and the Tombstone Milling & Mining Company increased its pro-duction. It had produced ninety thousand dollars per month in ore, but was now producing in excess of one hundred thousand per month, using thirty stamp-mills. The third dividend of fifty

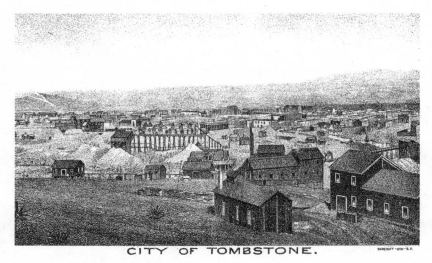

CITY OF TOMBSTONE.

City of Tombstone illustration, 1881, from the author's collection.

thousand dollars was paid on June 15, 1880, with many more expected, based on ore production.

Up in the hills behind Tombstone was a growing community of hoisting works, ore houses, offices, shops, private homes, and a boarding house—all to support the surrounding mines. The Toughnut mine had two sets of hoisting works, while the Girard had three. In late September, the Toughnut mill produced two bars of bullion, weighing 330 pounds, according to its shipper, Wells, Fargo & Co. The bullion was valued at $5,803.13. The Empire also had three sets of hoisting works, in addition to offices and waterworks. Just below all these mine enterprises, on a mesa near Empire Hill, sprang up a little town called New Boston.

With Tombstone's mines producing high volumes of silver ore, most presumed it was just a matter of time before it would have its own railroad depot. However, until that time, the newest railroad station at Benson, about twenty-eight miles away, was completed. The trip took nearly five and one-half hours, less than half the time it took from Tucson. With this addition, the stages changed their departure schedules. H. C. Walker's line departed Benson immediately after the train arrived, carrying passengers, Wells, Fargo & Co.'s treasure box, and light baggage. John D. Kinnear's stage immediately followed H. C. Walker, but only hauled heavy freight and express items. Walker's stage departed Tombstone at 5:00 p.m., allowing passengers to connect with the train in Benson. Kinnear's also had a stage departing Tombstone, but it left at 2:00 p.m. While Mr. Kinnear was busy driving stage-coaches, Mrs. Kinnear kept busy, too. She was engaged in prospecting in the Whetstone Mountains. The *Epitaph* reported Mrs. Kinnear and a lady companion were seen daily in the mountains with picks in hand searching for their great bonanza.

An anonymous letter to the *Arizona Daily Star* reported, "Improvements on every hand are visible. Tombstone is moving right on and shows a nervous energy and a fixed faith than ever before. It is this faith that is making Tombstone." The writer went on to say, "The greatest drawback is the water, this being entirely supplied by carts, but the pipes of the Sycamore Springs Water Company have been laid to within the city limits."[22] It was also in mid-July when the Western Union Telegraph line reached Tombstone, to great excitement.

Certain implements were a necessity in a mining community, and while picks, shovels, and axes were more or less safe to leave lying about, explosives were not. City council members decided to enforce this train of thought with a new city ordinance. Ordinance number eleven regulated keeping gunpowder and other explosives in town. The ordinance covered gunpowder, giant powder, dynamite, nitroglyc-erin, and all other highly explosive substances. These materials were allowed to be kept within the limits of the village of Tombstone, but only in such quantities and in such manner as the ordinance provided. No one could keep any such explosive weighing more than twenty-five pounds in total. Any such explosive had to be kept in a container of tin, iron, zinc, or any other noncombustible receptacle. Any and all containers had to be marked, kept in plain sight, and not be in danger of being ignited. Violators were fined up to fifty dollars and had their explosives confiscated.

With the town a little safer, *Arizona Quarterly Illustrated* said, "The streets are regular and the whole place laid out, and from the style and character of the buildings and business houses, there is an air of permanence and substantiality rarely noticed in a new mining camp. This is a quiet and peaceable community, and families are settling here and improving the moral atmosphere."[23]

Some may have claimed that Tombstone was a "fast city" with fast ways. If they were talking about the driving practices of those in town, they were right. Some citizens believed that the practice of fast driving through a crowded thoroughfare like Allen Street should be condemned. There were several instances of recklessness, and many wondered if there was a town ordinance governing speed. If so, who was supposed to be enforcing it, they wondered.

Tombstone had been covered in the national press, not because of its killings, but because of the silver mines. The *Epitaph* ran a story that appeared in the *San Francisco Bulletin* and then in Tucson's papers. The writer, who had recently paid a visit to the frontier mining camp, said, "The name Tombstone promises to become, so far as the city is concerned, a veritable monument in literature."[24] He also claimed the new weekly arrivals averaged one hundred. Town lots were in good demand, and houses, stores, and shops were quickly built. Many were exuberant about the rapidly rising town, but some remained skeptical about just how long the bonanza would last. Mining experts agreed that since more than a dozen mines had shafts down three hundred feet, and in almost every case they were extracting the best grade ore, Tombstone was safe. The Contention, thought to be the greatest mine in America, was producing forty thousand dollars per week. With the majority of the mines facing a promising future, the only concern was where to crush, or stamp, the ore. Only forty-five stamp mills were in operation—hardly sufficient for the existing development. Many mine owners started erecting mills, bringing the count up to nearly one hundred. A new custom mill was built at Contention. Once completed, it had a capacity of twenty-five stamps. The cost of the mill was about one hundred thousand dollars. A great convenience, it was also a good source of revenue for its owners.

Because of Tombstone's rapidly growing population, one Tombstonian offered a bet of one hundred dollars that the town's population would near fifteen thousand a year from July 1880. His bet was met with jeers from the crowd of sporting men who said, "He must be looking for a sure thing," and that they were "not in the habit of going against a skin game."[25] It's a good thing no one took his bet, because Tombstone's population never reached fifteen thousand. It reached its peak at about seven thousand in 1883.

The increasing population caused concern for those in need of water, which was in short supply. However, the Sycamore Springs Water Company was in the process of relieving this worry. By early August, they were well on their way to supplying Tombstone and nearby mining facilities with an abundance of water. They began by supplying the town's water in carts while the street mains were laid.

Customers desiring water at their residences were required to pay the necessary conduit fee and had meters placed as well.

Even with all Tombstone's conveniences, residents could not solve the awful problem of flies buzzing about town. It was hardly a situation Tombstone could eliminate, so the town tried to reduce the number of buzzing bandits by keeping the streets clean. Unfortunately, keeping the streets clean was a constant problem. It was so bad, the *Epitaph* often called the attention of the town's officials to the condition. On August 3, 1880, the *Epitaph* published this poem.

Owe, the Fliz!
Oh, the flies! The horrible Flies!
Buzzing around like election lies;
Dodging about like a maniac's dream,
Over the butter, and into the cream;
Holding convention all over the bread,
Biting your ears and tickling your head.
Crawling,
Buzzing,
Too busy too die—
Dog-gone the nasty, pestiferous fly.
— *Argonaut*

While the townspeople had to contend with the fly, the miner had it much worse. In addition to annoying surface conditions, underground work was difficult, dirty, and dangerous. Mining was a dangerous occupation. When accidents occurred, the danger level rose even higher. One miner proved very lucky when he dropped his candle and kicked it into a stack of explosive cartridges. The cartridges were quickly pushed against the side of the mineshaft and then exploded. The miner was fortunate to escape with just a few bruises around his head.

With so many miners and so many capitalists in town together, it was just a matter of time until hostility erupted. The miners disliked the capitalists because they were the men in charge, moneyed, and did not have to do a hard day's work. They were referred to as "money bags and mahogany tables." An article in the *Epitaph* pointed out, however, that without these capitalists, the workers would not have jobs. The writer even went so far as to say, "What would all the efforts of Gird or Schieffelin, great and deserving as they are, have amounted to had not their toils and struggles been supplemented by capital?"

The writer asked the laboring man to ease off the "money bags and mahogany tables."[26]

Tension between mine owners and miners grew when thirty-five men were discharged from the Toughnut mine on August 11. The men were let go because ore production greatly exceeded the mill's capacity to crush it. Also on the eleventh, the superintendents of many large mines posted a continuous notice in the paper to the miners. It stated, "Having established wages in this camp upon a scale more liberal than exists in any mining district elsewhere, we claim the right to employ such men as we see fit . . . we have given instructions to our foremen in the several mines operated by us to give employment to no one identified with the so-called 'Miner's Union.'" The miners responded by sending a letter to the *Epitaph* editor. It stated, "Having seen a notice in your paper August 12 in regard to the miner's union, in reply we would say that we do not propose to dictate to any mining company who they shall employ, or how they shall work their mines. Our object is mutual benefit to our members, to take care of our sick, bury our dead, and assist the widow and orphan. We would also say that the article of August 12 misrepresented the objects of the Union in every respect." It was signed, "Many Miners."[27]

Miners were not the only people concerned with mining affairs. The townspeople, capitalists, business owners, and stockholders also held an interest in what happened beneath Tombstone's and other mining surfaces. One such person was J. Murray Bailey, a stockholder in the Arivaca Milling & Mining Company. He wrote a letter to the secretary of the Arivaca, L. H. Thomas, regarding his concern in their mining property and responded to an inquiry about selling the mill.[28] Mr. Bailey was not in favor of selling the mill because he believed, with the right backing and workers, the property would be quite valuable. If the mills were sold now, the investors would lose money, he felt. He was, however, willing to sell his share at a fair value of five thousand dollars to anyone interested. If the mill proved profitable, that offer would be revoked.

A different perspective on Tombstone's lifestyle came from Reverend William Hill, who paid a visit to the silver city. In his report to Bishop J. F. Spalding of the Episcopal Church of Los Angeles, he advised he would give as correct an opinion as possible of Tombstone, as was in his power.[29] He sought neither to give a more rosy hue, or darker color, than present facts and future prospects warranted. In the reverend's report, he noted Tombstone's appearance and compared it to California mining towns twenty-five years past, with its sprawling features. He also said

> There is the same mushroom appearance of the buildings, the same reckless characters, making day and night hideous. The same almost unlimited gambling and drinking; the same absence of families, and the same disregard for God's holy day; I suppose there are at least sixty places of business there, and I could hear of but *two* that closed their doors for an hour on Sunday. Here too, the strange woman whose steps take hold on hell, plies her woeful trade, and many are her victims who should live a sober, righteous, and godly life.

He did note the Methodists were in the process of building a church. If Tombstone blossomed like it was supposed to, families would come, and Tombstone would be saved.

Although Tombstone offered many enticing things, one had to work in order to pay for them. In October, a list of wages and the cost of goods was produced for Tombstone.[30] While wages were good in Tombstone, the lack of materials hindered the employment process. Nonetheless, carpenters, blacksmiths, masons, and engineers earned six dollars per day, while miners earned four dollars, and laborers earned three dollars per day. Cooks earned from fifty to seventy-five dollars per month. The price of silver at this time was $1.20 per ounce.

With the price of silver as high as it was, more mining claims were being patented than ever before. On November 13, 1880, Wyatt, Virgil, and James Earp, along with Robert J. Winders, applied for a patent to the 1st North Extension of the Mountain Maid mine. The mine had a twenty-six-foot shaft and had three buildings, each about fourteen by thirty-four feet in size. This mine bordered the Yreka, Mattie Blaylock, and the Lala Rook.

Tombstone resident and *San Diego Union* correspondent Clara Brown wrote a letter that summed up the end of 1880. It began,

> Christmas was observed as a general holiday, most of the mines stopping work, which is not the case on Sundays. The writer and husband celebrated by a thirty-mile horseback ride over the surrounding country, to take in the settlements of Charleston and Contention, and the Contention stamp

mill, on the San Pedro River. The mill was running, and one who observes the action of its powerful machinery can but realize the importance of the mine that has paid $600,000 in dividends within seven months, whose stock is worth $80 per share.

She concluded, "Further development of many of the many claims is productive of the most gratifying results. Those skeptics who predicted the speedy failure of Tombstone mines find their forebodings as yet unrealized."[31]

1881

Arizona Quarterly Illustrated ran a story early in 1881, which outlined Tombstone's larger mines' progress. About the Contention mine they wrote, "The merits of this great, rich mine are well-known in mining circles. As a perfect piece of mine engineering, systematic work, and thorough development, no property in Arizona to-day is its superior. The record this mine has for itself, before the world, is hard to be equaled... There are few mines in the Territory so regular or uniform in value or character as this has been from the beginning."[32] They made similar comments about the Head Center, Sulphuret, Tranquility, Girard, Toughnut, and Goodenough mines.

While most reports regarding Tombstone were of a positive nature, there were some who remained skeptical, and possibly envious. The *Mining & Scientific Press* ran a story in February regarding the economical conditions in Tombstone. It was said Tombstone was "overdone," and, "In population and business, Tombstone is as top heavy as Uncle Sam's army, with its numerous generals. This at first glance is evident to the observant stranger who comes to spy out the country and rate the business prospects and the social aspects of the place. There are probably 1,000 or 1,200 structures of all grades fringing the streets here, while the inhabitants must number at least 3,000 to keep within approximate bounds. Now this is a large population for a place not affording steady employment to more than 400 miners."[33] They believed Tombstone was a year ahead of the mines in terms of ore production. The writer, identified only as J. D. P., said, "In consequence there are many idle, who, had they remained in their former localities might have employed their physical capital to greater advantage than they have here... I would not encourage miners of any grade to come here to look for work by the day exclusively, and the same applies with equal force to other orders of labor, such as clerks, bookkeepers, shopmen, lawyers...for here there are already enough and to spare." He concluded with, "But if men have some means and prefer to turn prospectors, and range amid the hills and mountains in search of hidden treasure, I say to all such that here is room for enough for all who come of this class, and they may be expected to find greater and more certain reward for their labor than they could, in perhaps, any other such country on the globe."[34]

A contrasting article appeared in the May *Engineering and Mining Journal* regarding Tombstone. Professor William P. Blake's article offered a bright future for Tombstone, and gave ore production figures for the larger mines. According to Blake, Tombstone was a town blessed with bounties both below and above the surface. Water and timber provided no great obstacle, and the climate was superb. Blake also wrote a report for the Way-Up Mining Company later in December. His report was done at the request of the company, for their stockholders. In it he wrote, "I believe that the vein will preserve the same characteristics along its course through the Way-Up and that it may be followed as it has been. The ore will be found to vary in its amount and value as the vein intersects different strata. When it cuts the shales I expect the gold content will be higher than when the lode intersects limestone."[35]

The Tombstone Milling & Mining Company (TMM), which first began with the Schieffelin brothers and Richard Gird, was now a large conglomerate. TMM's holdings now included the Toughnut, Surveyor, Goodenough, Lucky Cuss, Tribute, West Side, East Side, East Side No. 2, Owl's Nest, Owl's Last Hoot, and the Defense. These properties and others had produced seven hundred thousand dollars in dividends during the preceding fourteen months. The Western Mining Company's claim, the Contention, paid its stockholders nine hundred thousand dollars in dividends as of May 1881. The company's mill output for April was $144,000 from eighteen hundred tons of ore. The Grand Central, whose owners were mainly from Ohio and Chicago, was located south of the Western Mining Company. The Grand Central's mill return for April was $116,000.

While silver ore was an important find, determining how much one's discovery was worth was just as important. The simple discovery of silver ore didn't always bring wealth. To determine how rich one's discovery could be, it was necessary to have some ore samples assayed. A miner took his sample to the nearest assayer's office to

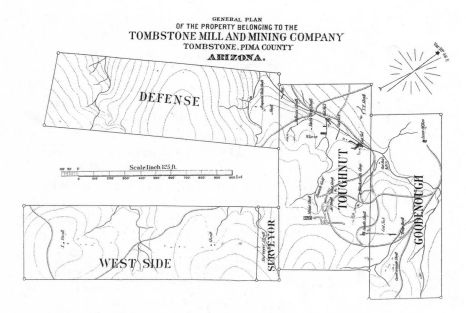

Tombstone Mill and Mining Co. map, courtesy of the Arizona
Historical Society.

determine the value. The cost of having ore assayed depended upon
what the ore contained. The cost for one silver assay was two dollars
while the cost of a copper assay ran five dollars. One assayer and
chemist in town, Henry Kearsing, also gave discounts for large assays
and taught assaying on the premises at reasonable terms.

"That the future of Tombstone is a bright one, anyone accustomed
to look beneath the surface will freely admit," began an article in the
Daily Nugget.[36] The report pointed out the many reasons why residents had faith in their camp's longevity. To begin, water had been
struck in the lower levels of the Sulphuret mine. Its owners proposed
to use the water to run mills in Tombstone, rather than export their ore
to the mills along the San Pedro River. The *Nugget* was also optimistic
after the best mining experts in the field, who projected the ore bodies went below the water level, inspected many of the larger mines.
The *Nugget* was even so bold as to compare Tombstone to the
Comstock Lode.

Tombstone's "croakers" claimed the end was near because water
had been hit in the mines and a few men were discharged from the

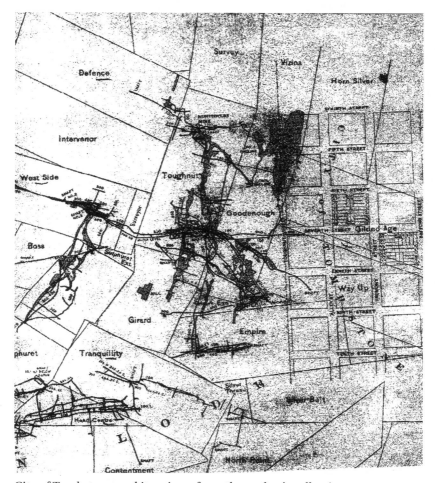

City of Tombstone and its mines, from the author's collection.

Contention mine. The *Nugget* combated the rumors by saying there were already plans to use the water from the mines and that men were let go at the Contention because fewer were needed to keep the mills running. The *Nugget* also stated, "Tombstone is today the most promising, and also paying, as its bullion output shows camps west of the Rocky mountains, and time will prove it."[37]

Tombstone's future was very promising, and even the business directories concurred with the *Nugget's* observations. *McKenney's Business Directory* characterized Tombstone as "One of the liveliest

Pacific slope towns." They also said, "The population is the most peaceable and hospitable that ever a stranger met with; and it is seldom that any crimes are committed in this place, rumors to the contrary notwithstanding."[38] The directory also noted that Tombstone had numerous hotels, lodgings, restaurants, and all the luxuries one found in San Francisco. They, too, projected that some of Tombstone's mines would last for years.

The mining industry required many tools to be successful, including explosives. In early August a new explosive was introduced into the Arizona Territory. The powder was called Vigorit, and had been successfully used in Virginia City, Nevada, and Bodie, California, mines. Jack Hays Jr., son of the infamous Texas Ranger and Indian fighter, arrived in town to interview mine owners about the new powder. Many said if the powder worked as was claimed, it would prove invaluable to the development of the district.

As talk of a new powder echoed, the Girard mine was temporarily shut down to erect a quartz mill. The mine itself was producing well, and having its own crusher allowed the company to reduce ore with a fair profit, if the ore could be reduced at a cost of twelve dollars per ton. Other mines around Tombstone still produced a fair amount of ore, despite minor setbacks. By the end of July, the large mines in town had yielded $432,906.31. Developers at the Grand Central had problems getting to the depth they wanted, and the Head Center was hung up for eight days because of a breaking reservoir, which reduced the ore shipment and yield of bullion. In spite of this, the ore in stopes and winzes of Head Center showed improvement in quality.[39] Vizina Consolidated mines were down to a depth of 333 feet, and about twenty-four tons of ore were being shipped daily. The Anchor mine made rapid progress and showed a promising future. One thing said about good mines was, "Money, pluck, and good management is what tells in a developing mine."[40]

Miners and businessmen alike were upset with Tombstone's city ordinance prohibiting carrying concealed weapons in town. The *Nugget* wrote a stinging article claiming it was the given right of Americans, by our forefathers, to carry firearms. They stated there were numerous ways to carry firearms that might not come under the mayor's ban. Despite the ordinance, Spangenberg's Gun Shop did brisk business with those in need of a good pistol, shotgun, ammunition, or anything else having to do with firearms. Spangenberg also offered his patrons a place to test their purchases. He opened a gun range in the back of his store for customers and sporting folks as well. The best marksman, or "boss shot," at Spangenberg's was Deputy Sheriff Billy Breckenridge, having shot twelve bull's-eyes in a row.

Once the summer rainy season arrived, observers reported that the creeks and springs in the Dragoon, Huachuca, and neighboring mountain ranges were abundant. Wildflowers flourished from the welcomed rains. One had to walk only a few minutes out of town to pick a variety of them. The *Daily Nugget* reported this was a "queer country where winter is spring, the spring, summer, and summer all the year round."[41]

Some of the summer storms were so violent that small camps established around Tombstone were completely washed away. The little hamlet named Mason's Camp did not stand a chance against Mother Nature's wrath, when a sudden cloudburst dumped torrents of rain, causing a sandy wash to fill with high, rushing water. Residents quickly found higher ground, but could save nothing of their community. They watched helplessly as their homes disappeared in the rush of water.

One summer day Tombstone experienced a storm that caused considerable damage. Heavy rain began at five o'clock in the afternoon and continued until about nine o'clock that evening. Within an hour of the rain falling, miniature rivers flowed where once dry-arroyos had lain empty. Summer weather was not always so devastating, and often afforded beauty. On another afternoon, Tombstone residents enjoyed a rare glimpse of a double rainbow. Lasting for an hour, it stretched from Contention Hill to the Dragoon Mountains.

During the "monsoon season," roads leading in and out of Tombstone were nearly washed away. Repairs took several days. Daily life was hampered, and stages could not get through with mail delivery, supplies, or even passengers. Mining operations were also affected; heavy quartz teams could not get ore to the mills along the San Pedro River.[42] During the monsoons, rain accumulated so quickly, boxes flowed down the city streets. The precipitation was accompanied by crashing thunder, strong wind, and dangerous lightning. Businesses and houses also felt the effects of the "monsoons" that pounded Tombstone, as awnings were ripped away and adobe buildings suffered "wash-out" damage.

Tombstone made it through the violent summer storms with minimal damage and readied itself for the fall. The *Daily Nugget* reported, "The days of cooling beverages and ice cream are about over for this

Loading ore, 1880s, reproduced by permission of the Arizona Historical Society.

season . . . Summer is non est . . . with regal steps and royal air . . . departs our Summer queen."[43]

On October 1, 1881, an article about Tombstone appeared in the *Mining & Scientific Press*. The article explained where Tombstone was, how it got its name, and who discovered it. It also reported that Tombstone's mining prospects were growing. At the time of printing, the town had fourteen steam hoisting works, six horsepower hoisters, and seven stamp mills, for a total of 125 stamps. These stamps were found at the Grand Central, Contention, Head Center, Boston & Arizona, Hopkins, and the Tombstone mines, including the one called "Gird Mill," and the other called "Corbin." The total bullion output for the end of August was a staggering $433,836. The Tombstone Milling & Mining Company, which employed 210 men, shipped four bars of bullion weighing 743 pounds. It was valued at $10,355.97 and was shipped by Wells, Fargo & Co. in late September.

Mining was a hard and dangerous business, and the men who worked in the mines risked their lives daily. James Tully, who resided in Nevada before coming to Tombstone, was employed at the Grand Central mine. While doing his job, he placed guides in a new shaft at a depth of about twenty feet from the surface. Ready to come up, he

Tombstone prospector postcard (date unknown), from the author's collection.

gave the necessary signal. The engineer, Stevens, thought Tully was down at least one hundred feet and turned on a full head of steam to bring him up. Before he could gain control of the brakes, the cage was carried up into the sheaves. Tully yelled at Stevens to stop, but it was too late. Thinking he could save himself, Tully jumped from the cage and fell to the ground. As he struggled to stand up, he slipped and tumbled down the shaft some 250 feet to his death.

A great amount of hard work and persuasion went into procuring investors from the East for the mining industry. So when individuals tried to dupe potential investors, it's understandable that legitimate prospectors were angered over such tactics. The practice of taking mineral of high grade from developed mines and using it in the East to sell undeveloped property was a typical swindle. Prospectors who were on the up and up frowned on this because it gave them a bad name and made the sale of good mines even more difficult.

Because the Tombstone papers circulated back East and often contained mining terms, the *Nugget* ran a story that explained what a "vein" or "lode" meant. It stated, "A vein or lode authorized to be located in a seam or fissure in the Earth's crust filled with quartz, or some other kind of rock in place carrying gold, silver, or other valuable mineral deposits named in the statute. It may be very thin, or it may be many feet thick, or irregular in thickness, and it may be rich or poor, provided it contains any of the metals named in the statute. But it must be more than detached pieces of quartz or mere bunches if quartz not in place."[44]

Mine owners in Tombstone were proud of the bullion they produced, and to show off their precious metals, many donated refined bullion specimens to the Soloman Lodge No. 1, F. & A. M. (Free and Accepted Masons). The lodge used the bullion pieces in ceremonial rites. Manufactured and engraved by local jewelers Hartmann & Voss, the twelve-piece set of "jewels" was a dazzling sight. Adolph E. Hartmann did the casting and workmanship, while twenty-one-year-old Otto C. Voss executed the engraving.

Many Tombstonians were known for penning their own poems for various occasions. One poem, entitled "Midnight Music," appeared in the *Epitaph* on the morning of October 26, 1881.

> I feel so awful jolly when the band begins to play;
> The music seems to sweeter sound after the close of day!
> When the fairy maiden lingered awaiting for the key;
> Whilst I wrote my loving letters to friends beyond the sea;
> I little thought the Atkins boy would give the thing away;
> And bring that thundering band around to fill me with dismay;
> But he's a jolly joker, and he knows a thing or two;
> And twigged my little game before I cast a shoe;
> Hereafter, when I borrow keys from friends upon the streets;
> I'll ask no spreeing cuss to keep the secrets of my sheets!

Although this jovial little poem graced the morning paper of the twenty-sixth, the next morning's paper was filled with grim details of the street fight that changed Tombstone's history. It was on this day that a series of events finally came to a violent end in the streets of Tombstone. October 26, 1881, was the day when Wyatt, Virgil, and Morgan Earp, along with John "Doc" Holliday, faced the Clantons and the McLaurys in a vacant lot behind the O.K. Corral. Even though the gunfight was between the Earps and Doc Holliday and the Clantons and the McLaurys, it affected the entire town.

Despite Tombstone's tumultuous atmosphere and Indian scares, the mines and miners worked hard on the hills and underground. The Tombstone Milling & Mining Company shipped three bars of bullion, weighing 831 pounds, and valued at $11,653. Still, there was talk, regardless of the bullion shipped from Tombstone, that this "boom town" would not last. Much to the surprise of those from the east and west coasts, Tombstone's mines were now at a depth of five hundred to seven hundred feet below the surface. There was actually an increase, rather than diminution in the quality and quantity of the ore. The total bullion yield for the past six months, April through September, was $2,741,673.49.

The mines employed many people who called Tombstone home. The Grand Central employed 90, the Contention 102, Tombstone mine 200, and the Vizina had 50. The number of men employed at the principal mines totaled 637. That total number did not include approximately one hundred more who did contract and assessment work.

While mining *could* be profitable, the cost of extracting the ore and hauling it to the mills was costly. The Contention, Grand Central, and Tombstone mines each shipped twenty-seven hundred tons of ore to the mills. The cost of hauling the ore averaged about three dollars per ton depending on the mine's location. The cost of hauling the ore to the mills and an increased water supply led many mine owners to erect mills near their mines. Many even projected they could mill ore for a profit, averaging twelve dollars per ton.

The *Harper's New Monthly Magazine* reporter who visited Tombstone in late November made this observation: "The small city, two years old at the date of this journey, had attained a population of 2,000, and property valuation, apart from the mines of $1,050,980. A desirable lot on Allen Street, between 4th and 6th, such was the business-like nomenclature used already in this settlement of yesterday—was worth $6,000. A shanty cost $50 to build, rented for $15 a month...On a commanding hill close by, to the southward, were the Toughnut and Contention, with above them many others discovered later. The larger mines have extensive buildings of wood, painted Indian red, with handsome draughting and assaying rooms within, and regularly educated scientists, etc...laborer above ground earned $3.50, and below ground $4, for a 'shift' of eight hours work; and the work went on night and day, Sundays and all. The outskirts consisted still of huts and tents. A burly miner could be seen stretched upon his cot in his windowless cabin barely large enough to contain it."[45]

Until now, Tombstone's main liability was its lack of water. However, with the addition of the Huachuca Water Company, Tombstone attracted even more hopeful fortune seekers. Tombstone resident Clara Brown wrote, "More capitalists are here than at any time heretofore, and they are manifesting a lively interest in the mining property by which we are surrounded."[46] The manager of Huachuca Water Company advised the newspaper of its progress on December 2, 1881. He stated a dam in Miller's canyon, in the Huachuca Mountains, was almost complete, and when done, its reservoir capacity would reach three million gallons. He claimed the conditions for storing water in the canyons was very favorable, and with a comparatively small amount of money, two hundred million gallons could be placed in the reservoirs. The extra flow of the springs in the canyons would vary during the seasons, except for in cases of extreme drought. If drought occurred, the water capacity would have been reduced to about one million gallons per day.

The water was delivered to Tombstone through a pipeline, which was under construction. The first of the reservoirs at the end of the pipeline was constructed on the Bon Ton mining claim, about three-fourths of a mile south of Tombstone, and about three hundred feet above it. It was thought the altitude of the reservoir was so great, the water could be flowed to any hoisting works or mill site in the district. The reservoir itself measured eighty by ninety by twenty feet, and capacity was 1,080,000 gallons. The reservoir capacity at the Tombstone end would be increased by twenty million gallons if the need arose.[47]

As the close of 1881 neared, Tombstone's citizens were proud of their town's progress. The *Epitaph* wrote, "It is safe to say that no other town in America, of its size and population, is better supplied in the way of amusements than Tombstone. Only last evening—which, by the way, was an extra quiet one—there were meetings of the firemen, the Odd Fellows, the city council, and the literary and debating society, together with a ball, a theater, a dancing school and a couple of private parties, all in full blast. Hurrah for Tombstone!"[48] The theater production was at Schieffelin Hall, where the Nellie Boyd company performed *Forget Me Not*.

Around this time, many of Tombstone's pro-Earp citizens involved in the Earp-cowboy hearing received anonymous threats upon their lives. Mayor Clum and even the presiding judge, Wells Spicer, had been threatened. Spicer placed a rather lengthy letter in the *Epitaph* defending his decision on the Earp trial, denouncing the cowards who sent threatening letters to him, as well as others. He said, "I am well aware that all this hostility to me is on account of my decision on the

Earp case, and for that decision I have been reviled and slandered beyond measure, and that every vile epithet that a foul mouth could utter has been spoken of me... that of corruption and bribery. It is but just to myself that I should hereby assert that neither directly nor indirectly was I ever approached in the interest of the defendants, nor have I ever received a favor of any kind from them or for them. There is a rabble in our city who would like to be thugs, if they had courage; would be proud to be called cow-boys, if people would give them that distinction; but as they can be neither, they do the best they can to show how vile they are, and slander, abuse, and threaten everybody they dare to. In conclusion, I will say that I will be here just where they can find me should they want me, and that myself and others who have been threatened will be here long after all the foul and cowardly liars and slanderers have ceased to infest our city."[49]

Despite Tombstone's oddities, mine developers and investors came to visit the richest find in Arizona's history. Mr. C. H. Phillips and Mr. G. F. Thornton were given a tour of the Grand Central mine by its foreman, Mr. Shaughnesay. They were taken to the bottom, some 465 feet deep, and then to the second and third levels. The *Epitaph* reported Mr. Phillips was very much surprised at the magnitude of the works, both above- and below-ground. The paper wrote, "The developments of ore put it in the first rank among mines in the United States."[50]

The year of 1881, like a roller coaster ride, contained many ups and downs for Tombstone. At the start of 1881, its mines were producing superb ore, and the town grew rapidly. Just as things looked promising, a fire devastated half of the business district. Despite this, the town rebuilt, and Tombstone seemed to be recovering, until the street fight took place and divided its residents. After a long hearing, a verdict of not guilty was rendered, and life appeared to be returning to normal.

Then came the death threats, which ended with the attempted assassination of City Marshal Virgil W. Earp. As Marshal Earp crossed Fifth Street, from between the Oriental Saloon and the Golden Eagle Brewery, he was fired upon. He was shot in the arm and in the groin. Stray buckshot hit the Golden Eagle Brewery and passed over the heads of men playing faro. Earp was taken to the Cosmopolitan Hotel, where he was attended to by Dr. Goodfellow. While delivering supplies to Earp's room, George Parsons overheard Virgil saying to his wife, Allie, "Never mind, I've got one arm left to hug you with." Virgil did lose the use of his arm, but survived the shooting. With the assassination attempt and a lot of loud noise, Tombstone ended 1881.

Tombstone resident Clara Brown observed, "Nature has most bountifully paved the way for a permanent prosperity. But, while there is much to encourage the settlers in this new country, there is also an element of lawlessness, an insecurity of life and property, an open disregard of the proper authorities, which has greatly retarded the advancement of the place." She continued with, "The outlook for the camp is very favorable at the present time, and everyone seems in good spirits."[51] She also noted that stages arrived full daily, houses were in great demand, and there was a noticeable increase in business activities.

The *Epitaph's* report of mining bullion from November 1, 1881, to January 1882 also indicated Tombstone had done well. The output for the Toughnut group, which consisted of the Contention or Western, Grand Central, Head Center, Vizina, Ingersoll, Sunset, and several other underdeveloped mines, was $6,488,361. Even with the mines in their early stages, the dividend amount reached $2,895,000.

One of Tombstone's most persistent miners was popular photographer Camillus S. Fly. Since 1880, Fly had invested large sums of money in various mines in the community. He located mines in the Dragoon Mountains, just south of South Pass, and sunk a shaft about ninety feet deep, but it yielded no results. Elsewhere, he sunk a shaft on the outcroppings of copper and iron, about five feet down, where he hit a vein of red oxide and green carbonate. The vein was three feet deep, about 43 percent copper, and yielded twenty-five dollars worth of silver per ton.

1882

On the morning of January 26, 1882, Tombstone was blanketed in a snowy, peaceful, white shroud. However, later that evening, the ringing of a fire alarm disturbed the ambiance. At nine o'clock, a small blaze broke out in front of the New York Saloon and Coffee House. The lamp inside the transparent sign on the outer edge of the sidewalk flared up and then touched the awning. William Cuddy and other firemen quickly arrived on the scene and tore the awning down. They put the fire out before it could do any more damage.

The following day, the Girard mill was the main attraction in town, when its new mill began working. It had been in the building stages since October 1881 and was now complete. Citizens gathered around the mill to witness its first movements. The Girard mill was regarded as one of the best appointed in the district. The battery building was

44 by 50 feet long and was 36 feet tall. The pan and tank building was 54 feet wide and 90 feet long. The boiler and engine rooms measured 36 feet by 40 feet. The Girard mill was the first to use corrugated iron for roofing. The mill also had two boilers that measured fifty-four inches in diameter, were 16 feet long, and had forty-six three-and-one-half-inch tubes. The boilers were built by Prescott, Scott & Co. The engine room was supplied with an elegant Corliss engine built by Frazer & Chalmer of Chicago.

The history of Tombstone's mines up to this point had been a remarkably prosperous one. There were no major interruptions, and the flow of bullion had steadily increased since the first stamp dropped in the Gird mill in June 1879. Milling ore in large quantities was commonplace for many mines, including the Toughnut and Goodenough. Until this time, only two mines had hit water level. Hitting water was good in the beginning, but once the water became too powerful in its flow, no machine could pump it out fast enough. At the Sulphuret and Head Center mines, water flowed so rapidly, it was impossible to reach the ore below the surface. However, the ore above the water was very good and yielded over 90 percent of its contents in precious metal.

The Tombstone Milling & Mining Company (TMM) continued to surprise even the most optimistic speculators. The preceding March, TMM's manager was unsure where his week's supply of ore for the mills would come, but as work progressed, the ore ledges enlarged. Since that time, ore finds were numerous and extensive. TMM's manager and its owners were confident the mines would produce ore for at least two years and probably longer than that.

Mines were generally considered a dangerous place where hard work was done, but on March 16, the Head Center mine served as a social gathering place. Mr. Chris Batterman, an engineer, and Mr. Elliott, of the Head Center mines, planned to leave for San Francisco. Their many friends hosted a party in their honor. A space in the hoisting works between the main shafts was cleared. The area was tastefully decorated with flags and bunting, and the floor was smoothed and waxed. A platform was built for Tombstone's Italian string band, which played music for the gala. Dancing continued all night, except for a brief interruption for refreshments and again when an elegant supper was served at midnight. A notable moment at the party took place when many of Tombstone's ladies presented an elegant piece of jewelry to twenty-seven-year-old miner Tom Moore. He received this gift

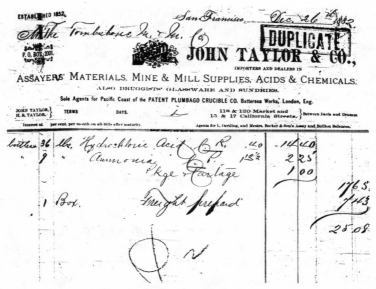

Invoice for mining supplies, 1882, courtesy of the Arizona Historical Society.

for being the wittiest gentleman of the party. Other gentlemen at the party were: Misters Eccleston, Bauer, Bourland, Vickers, Breckenridge, Wolcott, and McGinniss. Other guests included Mr. and Mrs. Julius Kelly, Mr. and Mrs. Frank Walker, and the Misses Colby, Brown, Santee, Rafferty, and Hartmann.

Just two nights after the Head Center party, a tragic event shook Tombstone. At 10:50 p.m. on March 18, 1882, Morgan Earp was shot. Despite warnings from many in town, Morgan went to Schieffelin Hall to watch *Stolen Kisses* performed by the Lingard Troupe. After the show, he headed toward Campbell & Hatch's Saloon and Billiard Parlor. His brother Wyatt met him on the street in front of the saloon.[52] As Wyatt approached Morgan, he said, "It's just a hunch Morg, but I want you to come along to the hotel and go to bed." Morgan said, "I want to have one game of pool with Bob Hatch. I promised I would play a game. It won't take that long. Then I'll go to bed." Before this conversation, Wyatt had been undressing in his room at the Cosmopolitan Hotel when a premonition of trouble cause him to get dressed and find his younger brother.[53]

Robert Hatch, an owner of Campbell & Hatch's Saloon and Billiard Parlor, was also at the theater that evening. He left the performance a little later than Morgan; they met at the door of his saloon. Wyatt followed Morgan into the pool hall and watched as his younger brother walk to the pool table in the back. He and Hatch began playing pool on newly covered tables. Wyatt rested on a chair sitting against the wall halfway down the room. Still feeling an uneasiness he could never describe, he got up and moved to a chair in the back of the poolroom, near Morgan.

With Bob Hatch watching carefully, Morgan leaned over to make a difficult shot. At that moment, two bullets, fired in rapid succession, crashed through the glass panel doors in the back of the saloon. Through the smoke, Wyatt watched as Morgan slipped to the floor. As he fell, Morgan tried to remove his gun from his holster, but was too weak. Wyatt ran to Morgan's side and asked, "Are you badly hurt, Morg?" Morgan replied, "Not badly, I guess." He looked down at his feet and said to Wyatt, "Take off my shoes, Wyatt." Wyatt took his shoes off, knowing Morgan did not want to die with his boots on. After all, he was not an outlaw. "Lay me straight, Wyatt." Wyatt just looked at him and said, "You are straight, Morgan. Just as straight as you can be." Morgan said, "Then my back is broken."[54] He was correct, as the bullet had entered on the right side of his abdomen, and passed through his spinal column, completely shattering it. The second shot just missed Wyatt, as it passed over his head and landed in the wall near the saloon's ceiling.

Morgan was taken to the cardroom in the saloon and placed on a lounge chair. His brothers, including Wyatt, Virgil, James, and Warren, along with Virgil and James's wives, and a few intimate friends, were at his side. They tried to get Morgan to his feet, but he said, "Don't, I can't stand it. This is the last game of pool I'll ever play."[55] From half past eleven until midnight, Morgan's mind was clear, and he spoke to his brothers. Morgan asked Wyatt if he knew who had shot him. Wyatt told him he did and that he would get them. Morgan replied, "That's all I'll ask, but Wyatt, be careful." Just after midnight, and on March 19, Wyatt's birthday, his brother passed away. Later that day, Morgan's body was sent home to Colton, California. The following day, Wyatt put Virgil and Allie Earp on the train and sent them to Colton for their own protection. Wyatt's older brother James stayed in town for a while, but on March 24, they sent their wives, Bessie and Mattie, to their California home.[56] Wyatt then set out to find the men who had killed his little brother. This began what is now known as Wyatt's Arizona vendetta. With the law on his side, he scoured the Arizona countryside looking for the outlaws. One by one, he found them. Most put up a fight and ended up dead. Wyatt eventually returned to California where he met up with his third wife, Josephine Sarah Marcus Earp. Together, they embarked on many projects and adventures until Wyatt's death in 1929.

The Grand Hotel welcomed General Sherman, who arrived in town on April 10. He and his party were taken on a tour of some of Tombstone's most productive mines. His first stop was at the Tombstone Milling & Mining Company's Toughnut mine, where he was taken to the three-hundred-foot level. Upon returning to the surface, his carriage took him to the Grand Central mine. The foreman took Sherman and his party down six hundred feet and then stopped at the three-hundred-foot level on the way back up. After lunch, they were taken to the Girard mill and shown the entire process, including how raw ore was converted to bullion. General Sherman and his party then retired to the Grand Hotel and rested before the ball that was held later that evening. Just before Sherman's visit, Wells, Fargo & Co. shipped three bars of bullion for the Tombstone Milling & Mining Company (TMM). They weighed 612 pounds, and were valued at $6,713. Two days later, on April 6, 1882, Wells, Fargo & Co. shipped three more bars for TMM, weighing 626 pounds and being valued at $7,247.

By late May, Tombstone was heralded by many across the nation for its mineral wealth. A story appeared in the *Epitaph* on May 20 that described the mining industry and the nation's mineral wealth. Tombstone was given a glowing review. The report described how Tombstone, just three years previous, had been only a lonely plateau. From a humble beginning of adobe huts and canvas tents, Tombstone had grown to fine architectural proportions. Its population had kept pace with growing fortunes, which had amassed to about four million dollars in dividends alone.

As business owners began to rebuild after Tombstone's second major fire on May 25, they were forced to follow stricter building ordinances. Ordinances were passed that regulated building materials, as well as prohibiting fire hazard materials within city limits, such as hay and dynamite.

A little over a week after the fire, the hum of hammers, pick shovels, and other building tools were heard throughout Tombstone. Residents removed old ruins and piled new adobe blocks and lumber on the streets where their businesses would be rebuilt again. Some businesses temporarily relocated to other sites while the foundations

Illustration of miners, 1881,
from the author's collection.

for their new buildings were laid. The Alhambra Saloon temporarily relocated on Allen, above Seventh Street, while its owners, Mellgren and Nichols, rebuilt their saloon.

As the city of Tombstone traveled the road to recovery, a near tragic event riveted the mining community. In early June, two miners at the Blue Monday mine were nearly suffocated to death, when they set off charges at the one-hundred-foot level in the mine. Anxious to see the results of their labors, they hastily descended back down the mine in a bucket on the windlass. The windlass operator did not receive the customary "all right" signal after the men reached their stopping point and suspected something was amiss. He then climbed into the windlass and, when he reached the one-hundred-foot level, saw the two miners lying on the ground, almost dead. He tied one of the men to the bucket and quickly ascended to the top. He brought the second man to the top using the same method. It took three hours for the men to regain consciousness once they reached the surface.

Many major mines and mills in Tombstone belonged to corporations that sold stock in their company and then paid out dividends. The Girard Gold and Silver Mining Company, one such corporation, held its annual stockholders meeting in Camden, New Jersey, on June 13, 1882. The board of directors reported the company's mill, which contained twenty stamps, was in good working order and crushed all the ore for their mines. The company's mines included the Girard,

Pima and Cochise County map, 1884, from the author's collection.

Sulphuret, Tranquility, and Contention. They also began crushing ore for other mines in the district, and made between ten and twelve thousand dollars each month by doing this. The company also owned the water power in the Tombstone vicinity and made a good profit from it. The Girard Company's receipts for 1882 were $171,378.92, with a balance of $156.46 in the treasury. The company's entire debt was placed at $78,121.40. Of 250,000 shares of stock offered, none were left unsold. The board of directors advised the shareholders that the company milled its own ore because it could not be produced fast enough in paying quantities.

Not only were the Girard Gold and Silver Mining Company's mines doing well, but so were most of the other mines in Tombstone. The *Epitaph* ran its weekly review of Tombstone's mines and also interviewed an experienced mining man from the county. He said, "Never have I seen a better showing throughout the district or heard a more confident tone among mining men." The *Epitaph* also reported three new significant strikes, including one in the Goodenough mine, where owners had struck a very large, promising body of ore, which steadily increased as miners worked it. The Randolph mine encountered a similar strike at the 118-foot level, and ore taken from this strike assayed at two hundred to twelve hundred dollars. Because of the large amounts of ore taken from the Randolph, Mr. J. Brewster, secretary of the company, made arrangements to erect a mill at the site.

Many miners, along with their superintendents, busily prepared for the Denver mining exposition in late June. A notice was placed in the paper calling for everyone who had mining claims in Cochise County to bring their best ore sample to the *Epitaph*'s office. Ore specimens from all the biggest mines in Tombstone were collected and displayed in a special cabinet at the exhibit. The Tombstone Milling & Mining Company supplied samples, as did the West Side mine, including a specimen that assayed 388 ounces in gold. Other samples were provided by the Ingersoll, Empire, Eden Lass, Luck Sure, Way-Up, Bradshaw, and Sunset mines.

There is no denying Tombstone's minerals were rich and valuable, but it was up to the assayers to determine just *how* valuable. One assayer was Tombstone pioneer Henry Kearsing. Henry had come to town in early 1880 and was considered one of Tombstone's top assayers. In addition to assaying ore for the mines in and around Tombstone, he contracted with various companies in other towns. He also taught others the skill of assaying—on reasonable terms.

Mining boomtowns drew all types of folks. Tombstone was no different. People of various religious affiliations, different occupations, and a wide array of nationalities called Tombstone home. It could easily have been called the "melting pot" of Arizona. A census of Cochise County, ordered by the legislative session to be taken, was completed in early July. They requested this census to determine proper representative appointments for the next legislative assembly. The Cochise County Board of Supervisors chose William "Billy" Breckenridge to handle the assignment. Breckenridge was appointed by Melville Leslie to conduct Tombstone's portion of the census.

The census results were promising with 9,647 people inhabiting Cochise County, and 5,300 residing in Tombstone. Of those in Tombstone, twenty-four different countries were represented. Topping the list were 2,880 Americans. Second were the Irish at 559, and the German population was 300. Nearby Mexico was also well represented with 423 inhabitants, and the Chinese totaled 245. There were approximately 200 Canadian natives, and about 200 of "her majesty's royal subjects." Fewer than one hundred residents each represented other countries, including Scotland and Austria. Natives of Norway, Sweden, Russia, Switzerland, Italy, France, Belgium, Portugal, Greece, Turkey, Australia, and Hindustan also lived in Tombstone. Other Tombstone residents hailed from the Hawaiian Islands, South America, and the West Indies.

Although most were pleased with the census results, not everyone was happy. A week after the census results appeared in the paper, an *Epitaph* article questioned its accuracy. The article said it was "nonsense" to believe there were only 5,300 people living in Tombstone, when clearly seven thousand people were residing within the city's limits. It further stated it was impossible to imagine Cochise County with any number less than fifteen thousand. In support of this, the article cited Tucson and Calabasas's census, which totaled seventeen thousand. How could Cochise County, with the towns of Tombstone, Bisbee, Charleston, Contention, Benson, Dos Cabezas, Wilcox, and a host of mining camps and railroad stations fall behind Pima county in census numbers? The writer said, "Surely, there has been a great neglect somewhere. Perhaps the census marshal did the best he could, but... the result works great injustice." Concern over the census numbers was understandable because the number representing Cochise County in the assembly was based on the census results.

On August 12, the *American Contract Journal* published a small piece on the history of Tombstone's waterworks. It described how Tombstone had had no water source itself, and how the Sycamore Springs Water Company was the first to deliver water to Tombstone. Their water came from the Dragoon Mountains, about eight miles from town. Next came the Tombstone Water, Mill & Lumber Company whose water supply came from a nearby stream at Watervale. It cost $1.50 per month to have water supplied to a residential dwelling and $2.50 for lodging houses. Bathhouses were charged $10.00, while barbershops paid $2.50. Livery stables on Allen Street paid the most, at $15.00, while the saloons paid a mere $3.00 for their water. The third supplier, Huachuca Water Company, was completed in July 1881. The Huachuca Water Company brought water from Miller's Canyon, between the two highest peaks in the Huachuca mountains, some twenty-five miles south of the city. A reservoir, 100 by 80 feet and 22 feet deep, held water at 1,000 feet above Tombstone. The water was collected from there, and distributed by a seven-inch wrought iron pipe down the canyon, across the San Pedro Valley, 1,900 feet lower than the source, and then up again, to another reservoir built in the rocks. This reservoir, 385 feet above Tombstone, was 90 by 80 feet and 20 feet deep. It was lined with stone masonry and floored with Portland concrete. At a total cost of five hundred thousand dollars, the Huachuca Water Company was able to deliver eight hundred thousand gallons of water to Tombstone daily, thus making it a safer and better place to live. Tombstone residents and business owners benefited from having these three water companies in town. Not only did they have the reliability of water, but rates were kept low because of the competition for business.

Despite saloon brawls, street scrapes, and the occasional unsavory character, Tombstone was a wealthy, sophisticated city. Its mines had, after all, produced bullion valued in the millions. The U.S. Mint Bureau even sent a representative to visit Tombstone's mines for a report to appear in its annual review. Mr. A. W. Lawler arrived in late October and stayed for several weeks to complete his report on Arizona's mineral wealth and the production of precious metals. Mine owners, superintendents of mines, and those having reliable information were encouraged to talk with Lawler. Lawler's report was extremely important to Tombstone, as it circulated throughout the United States and Europe. This was Tombstone's opportunity to tempt those who thought about investing in the mining industry.

Clara Brown noted Tombstone's society had improved since she first arrived in 1880. She penned, "Society is improving all the time. Gradually the standard of respectability has been raised, until now a lady can go 'into company' without coming into contact with, and thus treating as an equal, persons who would elsewhere be proscribed from the ranks of honest society."

Early November brought good news for Tombstone and its mines. Many had long hoped the water would be pumped from the depths of Tombstone's prosperous mines. The directors of the Contention Consolidated mines met in San Francisco, and plans were made to install water pumps in the mines. E. B. Gage and E. H. Wiley of the Grand Central Consolidated mines were also in town and met jointly to discuss the idea. It was finally agreed the pumps would be placed in the old works of the Grand Central, and once the pumps were sunk below the six-hundred-foot level, the water could be pumped out. Once the pumping began, water was carried to a level connecting with the Flora Morrison mine, and from there it was hoisted out of the mines. Only the Earth herself knew what treasures were buried below the six-hundred-foot level, but with the help of a little machinery, Tombstone was hoping to learn her secrets. The *Epitaph* said, "Should good ore bodies be found below the water level, and the indications are most flattering in that direction, the future of Tombstone will be insured for an indefinite period, and an era of prosperity, dawn upon it such as not yet experienced."[57]

Despite many prosperous saloons in town, they were not Tombstone's primary source of income. Tombstone's wealth was attributed to its richly successful mines. The richness was measured by the values of the bullion production for the year of 1882 from the larger mines and mills:

Contention	$ 1,580,542.13
Grand Central	$ 1,358,820.85
Boston Mill	$ 250,000.00
Knoxville/Stonewall	$ 1,500,000.00
Tombstone M & M	$ 1,440,895.00
Girard (own & custom ore)	$ 177,540.00
Head Center	$ 125,079.81
Watervale Mill	$ 15,000.00

In 1882, the mills produced, on average, about $433,155.44 per month using the above figures. According to the *Mining Record*, the county of

Cochise, including Tombstone, produced an estimated $4,775,000 in silver and $325,000 in gold. Tombstone ended the year with prosperous and sophisticated living, coupled with successful businesses, productive mines, and even limited telephone service.

At the end of the year, and in spite of Tombstone's progress and its prosperous mines, resident Clara Brown wrote, "If the value of the town lots were only as high as the real estate that circulates generously through the air, some of us citizens of Tombstone would experience equally exalted spirits. But stubborn facts show that the property sells, if it sells at all, at a ridiculously low figure...There are those who have every confidence in the future of the camp, and who consider the present depression but the 'calm before the storm,' or, in other words, boom."[58]

1883

Many people came to Tombstone with the hope of striking it rich—some did, some did not. Regardless of whether they found their fortune or not, most miners approached the search in the same fashion. They arrived in town with their tools, supplies, and most importantly, their determination. Come hell or high water, they were determined to find silver. Determination of that kind led to a major ore discovery in February 1883. Its discoverer was Charles Barber, who was a newcomer to Tombstone's silver boom.

Upon his arrival, Barber began working on an abandoned shaft once used at the Gilded Age mine. The mine was located on the northeast corner of Sixth and Allen streets. The local miners thought Barber was crazy for working on a mine abandoned by a large company, for surely if there were ore to be found, they would have found it. The *Republican* stated, "Those who worked on the Contention ore body made no bones in declaring that Barber would never strike ore there and gave for their reasons that the Tombstone company had run adrift up to almost the range of this shaft and had found nothing. That was the clincher."[59] Despite many negative comments, Barber continued his work, saying his mineral magnet indicated ore in the area at about 130 feet deep and he would find it. The locals called his magnet a "hoodoo stick" and laughed at him.

The Gilded Age's shaft was already down about one hundred feet, so Barber only had about thirty to fifty feet to go. He worked day and night shifts until one Wednesday afternoon, the workmen blew through the capping and discovered a rich ore deposit similar to that found in the Toughnut and Goodenough mines. The news of his strike spread like wildfire and created quite a stir in town. The next couple of days people visited the mine to see if, in fact, Barber had discovered silver. After visiting the mine, they were convinced of Barber's discovery.

When Tombstone resident and diarist George Parsons visited Chicago, he met with a *Chicago Daily Tribune* reporter who asked about the recent Indian outbreak in Arizona. George gave them an interview on April 7, 1883, which appeared in the April 8 paper:

> He describes Arizona as being wonderfully rich in deposits of the precious metals. Several bonanza mines have already been opened, and the attention of the capitalists has been called to others, which promise to be rich, but the troubles with the Indians are proving a serious drawback to the development of the Territory. This last outbreak he says, has put Arizona back another year and frightened away people who were preparing to settle there and make permanent investments.
>
> The difficulties now are with the Indians, the outlaws who infested this region having nearly all been driven away or overcome. The mining camp is situated between the San Carlos Agency on the north and the Sierra Madre Mountains in Old Mexico. Between the agency Indians and those in old Mexico there is constant communication, and they are continually inciting each other to commit depredations. Those living south of the border line cross over into United States Territory, and the San Carlos Indians go over into Mexico, committing all sorts of atrocities while on the war-path. Gen. Crook tagged the agency Indians, and one of them was killed a short time ago, which proves beyond a doubt that all the hostile Indians do not live south of the border line. Since I came north several of my most intimate friends have been killed by these savages.

The reporter asked, "Have you not soldiers and Gen. Crook to protect the country?" Parsons replied,

> We are supposed to have four companies of United States troops at Ft. Huachuca, a six-company post twenty-five

miles west of Tombstone. These soldiers are always about twenty-four hours behind time in following up a band of savages. The Indians make sallies, murder the whites, and are back safe and sound in their mountain retreats long before troops are ready to follow them. A short time ago five men were killed by the savages only seven miles from the post. Four companies of soldiers were ordered to start in pursuit at five o'clock in the morning, and it was five o'clock in the afternoon when they reached the scene of the massacre. Of course all the Indians had escaped. General Crook does not seem to be doing any better than his predecessors. He has never been subjected the Chiricahua Apaches, who live in Old Mexico, and are continually making hostile incursions into Arizona, keeping up a steady communication with the Indians on the agency. The latter are well provided with guns and ammunition. It has been the custom to have about twenty-five Indian scouts at the different posts. These devils are kept a few months, till they have been drilled in our ways, and then they are sent back to the agency and a new lot taken on. They steal our guns and ammunition, and then turn against us, and supply their neighbors. The officers would rather not have Indians for fighting-men, because they are so treacherous, but they are taken and drilled in accordance with orders from the government. Two or three of those supposed to be the most reliable are employed as trailers. The savage nature of these Indians is illustrated by the horrible deed committed by one of their scouts. He agreed with some of the officers at the post that if they would give him a certain number of cartridges he would bring in his own father's head. He went, and soon came back with the head, and then offered to bring in the old woman's, his mother's, if they would give him more cartridges. This is a specimen of the sort of soldiers these red devils make.

The reporter next asked, "Why do not the soldiers protect the people?" George replied, "I do not know. It is generally believed that money is being made out of the agencies. If the United States government would only withdraw all the troops in Arizona, and tell the settlers to take care of themselves, they would soon settle this Indian question. These bands of hostiles are small in number, and they could be disposed of, but so long as the soldiers remain, the people naturally look to them for protection. The Mexican government is willing to cooperate with ours in the subjugation of these savages, and if Mexico was like some of the great powers she would bring in big and just claims against our government for damages and depredations committed within her territory by our agency Indians. Arizona has a beautiful climate, and is one of the finest mineral countries. She will soon have ample railroad communication with the outside world. All that is needed now to develop her resources is protection against the Indians. The failure of government to subjugate these hostile tribes is a serious drawback to the welfare of the Territory." Parsons returned home to Tombstone; he was treated like a hero for being frank in his views of the Indian situation.

The dangers associated with mining were very real, as residents and miners were again reminded, when another mining accident occurred. The Contention Mine was the unfortunate host to this latest tragedy. Its victim was thirty-four-year-old James Lacy, a night shift boss who was a native of Ontario, Canada. During his shift, he hopped into the cage and was lowered to the first level. As he walked out of the cage, the car man on the second level gave the signal to lower it, not realizing Lacy was not clear. As the cage was lowered, Lacey was wedged between the bonnet of the cage and the station timbers. Because of Lacy's large size, the cage could not descend, and he could not escape the crushing effects of it. Once the miners realized what had happened, they brought Lacy to the top and raced him to the hospital. Dr. Goodfellow examined the miner and advised Lacy's niece that her uncle's chest was crushed and he would not survive. Much to Dr. Goodfellow's surprise, Lacy survived and resumed mining after his miraculous recovery. Lacy began mining in Tombstone in 1879. Before that he resided in Virginia City, Nevada, and had also spent time on the Pacific coast.

Previous longtime Tombstone resident and saloonkeeper, Thomas Corrigan, paid a visit to his old roost in late July 1883. In December 1881 Tom first left, and now he had come back to visit some old friends. Many were interested in his stories and were curious to know if he had found any silver in the Sierra Madre. Corrigan told his adventurous story to a *Republican* reporter. He began with, "You know, I left here under the engagement to the Santa Maria Mining Company in Sonora." He went on to say that after a seven-month stint with them, he, his brother, and Thomas Shanahan headed out for the Sierra Madres. They arrived at an old Mexican village called Teopre. The town, once laden with gold, had thrived a century earlier, until an overwhelming force of Apaches, under the leadership of Coronado, devastated the area. No one was left to tell the stories of this once-great haven. After two weeks of finding no silver or gold, they continued prospecting en route to Trinidad. About seventy-two miles later, they reached a very rich mine called the Father of Christ, owned by Dr. Alsure. Eight miles from that mine, they located an old abandoned mine called the Compañero and denounced it. Continuing their journey, they finally reached a site about sixty miles down from the Yaqui River. They opened a mine site, but were only able to extract ore that assayed at about seventy-five dollars per ton. They remained at this site until December 1882, but gave up on it and returned to the Compañero site in January 1883. They began work on the site by digging tunnels and eventually sank a winze. Before his visit to Tombstone, they sunk another winze and had 250 tons of ore on a dump waiting to be milled. Tom's ore assayed at one hundred dollars per ton, and he felt confident he could amass the fortune he desired. In addition to good ore, Tom spoke highly of the land and said it was abundant with woods and water that had large game, such as deer, turkey, and bear.[60]

Tombstone's mines and mills were still producing good quality ore and turning it into bullion. During the month of July 1883, the Contention mill reduced 2,015 half tons of ore, which produced twenty-five bars of bullion. The bullion was valued at $72,132.33. In August, it reduced 441 half tons of ore, producing five bars of bullion with a value of $12,730.31. Unfortunately for the Contention's investors, a pillar block at the mill cracked, and it was forced to stop operations for twenty-five days, and "sixteen hours," according to the *Republican*. By late September, the crack was fixed, and the mill was once again crushing ore.

The Contention mine faced a much bigger challenge. As the miners worked on the four-hundred-foot level, they discovered a new body of ore on the regular ledge. It contained iron pyrites and black sulphurets, which were assayed at one hundred dollars per ton. The ledge also contained gold, which assayed at the same value. Finding the ore was one thing, but getting to it was quite another. The miners had to wait until the cement foundation was finished and water-pumping works were set in place. By October, the majority of pipes and timber supports were in place. When finished, the works pumped 450–500 gallons of water per minute to the surface.

The Grand Central's mine and mill also kept up its pace, and since March 1881, showed record bullion production of $2.8 million. In late September, it produced the largest "clean-up" of the season, which amounted to thirty thousand dollars. The *Republican* stated, "This is proof positive that business neither lags nor is falling off in this valuable property. We hear that in the drifts which are being run north of the new hoisting works some new developments have been made on the one hundred, four hundred, and six hundred foot levels, the latter being particularly rich and giving every confidence to the fact, and with a larger force of men in work, this property could be made to pay dividends yet before the end of the year."[61]

The year of 1883 was an anxious one when it came to mining matters. In early 1883, the mines had been dug as deep as possible, but were stalled because water filled the lower levels. The Grand Central was the first mine to install water-pumping equipment, which enabled them to explore mines at a greater depth. This worked at first, until a power problem shut the mine down again. It didn't start again until the Contention Company offered to share in the work. Contention Consolidated's mines had, in the first five months of 1883, produced 205 silver bars valued at $553,085.91. Because of their stoppage, they only produced thirty bars total for July and August, valued at $84,869.64, and were projected to produce $240,000 worth of silver for the rest of the year. Many other mines, including the Prompter and Tombstone Milling & Mining's holdings, encountered similar problems.

By the end of 1883, Tombstone had become the heart and soul of Cochise County, at least according to the *Republican*. It was a town where "the pulsation regarding mining matters emanated."[62] Despite many misgivings as to whether or not Tombstone would make it, its pulse was beating regularly. The crisis had passed in Tombstone, and it was now confidently considered a permanent mining center with a great future. No one denied 1883 was a tough, uncertain year for Tombstone, but by year's end, the town had slowly made its way back to a place where people felt they could safely invest capital.

1884

As another new year began, Tombstone residents saw an increase in mining production, which led to a renewed faith about its future. Residents were again beginning to feel confident in their town since the Contention mines were drained of 550,000 gallons of water, and work resumed on previously idle mines.[63] The ore output in early January had increased from late 1883, and there was every reason for hopefuls to believe the ore output would keep increasing.

An employee of the Contention Company, Frank Ruez, came to town in early January. Mr. Ruez had been enjoying the nightlife in Tombstone, and by late that evening was fully intoxicated. Bleary-eyed, he wandered to Tombstone's new Occidental Hotel, where he secured a room for the night. Shortly after retiring, Ruez raised an alarm, and one of the hotel's owners, Joseph Pascholy, went running. He entered Ruez's room and found him standing there, half dressed and complaining he had been robbed of eight hundred dollars in checks, some cash, and his watch. Pascholy examined the room and found no signs of forced entry. He was convinced no one had come into the room, save for Ruez. Ruez insisted he had been robbed, so Pascholy also searched his clothes. He discovered ninety dollars cash in Ruez's clothes, but there were no checks or watch. Mr. Pascholy told the *Republican* newspaper he was sure Ruez was not robbed. He also stated Ruez had probably given his checks to a friend to hold, but in his drunken state, failed to remember doing so.

Former Tombstone resident and Cochise County Sheriff John Behan's return to Tombstone in 1884 was less than a happy reunion. Shortly after arriving back in town, District Attorney Smith advised Behan of four outstanding indictments against him. Three of the indictments were for alleged irregularities in the accounts of ex-sheriff Behan, and the other was for failure to turn over a duplicate 1881 assessment roll to his successor. Since the monetary discrepancies were small, the district attorney settled out of court with Behan.

It had been almost six years since Edward Schieffelin discovered his first silver, and Tombstone had already produced $25,000,000 of bullion by mid-1884.[64] Tombstone had, in that short period, become preeminent among the mining districts in the territory. Ore bodies of such size had never been found in Arizona before, and they were easily worked. They yielded a 90 percent and upward return by the process of stamps, pans, and settlers. Tombstone's top producing mines had the most advanced machinery and immense pumps that were capable of handling the heavy water flow. There were more than three thousand mines located in the Tombstone district at that time.

On May 1, Tombstone's mining industry was brought to its knees. The mines and the mills were shut down because of a miners' strike. The miners made four dollars per day, but the mine owners wanted to

Tombstone Consolidated Gold & Silver Mining Co. stock certificate, 1880s, from the author's collection.

reduce their pay to three dollars. The miners refused to work for any-thing less than four dollars per day, so the mines remained idle for three months. A miners' union was formed to support the four dollars per day wage. This was, after all, comparable to the wages of bricklay-ers, carpenters, masons, engineers, and painters, but for much more dangerous work. The union appeared to gain strength for a while and was supported by unions in other mining communities like Bodie, California, Virginia City, Nevada, and others. Men in these unions sup-plied funds to the Tombstone miners so they could hold out and not give in to the mine owners.

The mine owners claimed they could not afford to pay the min-ers any more than three dollars per day until the water had been pumped out of the mines. This was hard for the miners to swallow, since there was a large quantity of low-grade ore available above the water level. Guards, including diarist George Parsons, were positioned at various mines day and night to ensure the miners did not damage the mines. Trouble was anticipated for a while, but once soldiers from nearby Ft. Huachuca arrived, the excitement began to subside. After about four months, the Miner's Union was dissolved, and the men went back to work.

After the strike, the Grand Central mine removed about 100–120 tons of low-grade ore, giving employment to about 180 men. Prospecting was closely watched as the third and fourth levels showed favorable results. New and larger pumps were constructed at the Grand Central and, when combined with those already in place at the Contention mine, were expected to control the water flow below the six-hundred-foot level. The Contention Company did not start its own operation for a couple more months because its ore, at about water level, was smaller than Grand Central's. It was, however, ready to run its pump when the Grand Central began. Even though the Contention was currently silent, it was still the leading mine in Tombstone. Since its discovery, the Contention had produced over $5,000,000 of bullion.

Over the years, Tombstone's mines, both small and large, had become part of a larger corporation. By the summer of 1884 Tombstone's top producing mines were consolidated under a hand-ful of large mining corporations. The Western Mining Company began in 1880, but was now under the Contention Consolidated Mining Company umbrella, along with the Flora Morrison and Sulphuret mines.

The Grand Central Mining Company, of Youngstown, Ohio, owned and controlled the Grand Central, Leviathan, Naumkeag, South Extension, Emerald, and other claims. They also owned two steam hoisting works capable of being sunk two thousand feet. The ore was shipped to the company's thirty-five stamp mill on the San Pedro River, ten miles west of Tombstone. Since the mill began in March 1881, it had produced over $3,000,000 in gold and silver bullion.[65] Once water pumps were installed, about one million gallons of water per twenty-four hours were pumped out of the mines. It was believed water in the mines lay only in large basins and, once removed, would no longer pose a threat to mining operations. By late October, the Grand Central mine employed 220 men. The pumps stalled in the Contention mine, however, once it was discovered the water was deeper than was first estimated.

The Tombstone Milling & Mining Company, a New York corpora-tion, was among the first to begin operations in Tombstone. By this time, the company owned eleven mining claims, which covered about 161 acres of land. The holdings included some of Edward Schieffelin's original mines—the Toughnut, Goodenough, West Side, and Lucky Cuss. The company had a smelter near its mill along the San Pedro River for working the tailings.

The Empire mine was owned by another large corporation, the Empire Company, from Boston. This mine adjoined the Tranquility, Girard, and Goodenough, and had two shafts. The mine's dumps had produced three thousand tons of ore, which were waiting to be crushed when the hoisting works resumed operation.

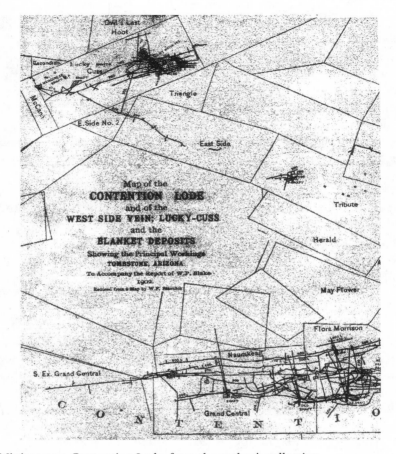

Mining map, Contention Lode, from the author's collection.

The Girard Gold and Silver Mining Company of New Jersey and the Boston & Arizona Smelting and Reduction Company of Massachusetts were still strong forces in Tombstone. The Girard Company, one of the oldest in town, had done the least amount of development work. It was said to be an excellent property with a large ore body. By mid-1884, thirty-six hundred tons of ore had been removed, averaging about sixty dollars per ton. An assay of the tailings showed them to contain forty-seven dollars per ton worth of silver. The Boston Company contained a twenty-stamp mill and a patented roasting furnace. These works, along with their Stonewall mine, had been worked diligently and produced heavy profits. Their mill, like the others, was located on the San Pedro River, between the towns of Charleston and Contention.

Other active mines in and near Tombstone included the Old Guard, Alps, Lima, Green Cloud, Bunker Hill, Manmouth, Rattlesnake, Ground Hog, Prompter, Way-Up, Empire, Gilded Age, Randolph, Mamie R., Ingersoll, and Bradshaw.

The cost of living in Tombstone, despite all the money made from the mines, was still somewhat higher than other Arizona cities. This was primarily because most things had to be imported. Consumers not only paid for the goods, but they also had to pay for the cost of transporting goods to town. For example, lumber could be bought in Prescott, Arizona, for twenty to thirty dollars per thousand, but in Tucson and Tombstone, and even Texas, it cost anywhere from forty to sixty dollars per thousand.

Wages in Arizona averaged about $40 per month, depending upon one's trade. Clerks made $50 to $75 per month; teamsters earned $40 to $60 per month; farm laborers and herders earned $30 to $40 monthly; and day laborers earned from $2.50 to $3.50 per hour. All wages included board. With the exception of meat, flour, and vegetables, nearly everything else either consumed or worn in Tombstone was imported. The cost of coffee was twenty cents per pound, tea cost fifty cents to one dollar per pound, and sugar ran twenty cents per pound. Room and board cost anywhere from $6 to $9 per week, or a single room could be rented for $10 to $20 monthly. If one wanted to rent a three- or four-room house, it cost $15 to $25 per month. A suit of clothes could be purchased for about $15, and a pair of boots cost $4 to $7. Other articles of clothing, like a hat, ranged from $1 to $4.[66]

Diarist George Parsons summed up how most people probably felt about Tombstone, with his December 31, 1884, entry. "Last day of the old year... Well, I wonder what Dame Fortune has in store for me the coming year. I said upon leaving California for Arizona and a mining life that I would try it for five years, and the five years are nearly up. I think that a little more perseverance will win me the day, and I shall stay with the present mining enterprise to the bitter end and probably decide things by this test."[67]

1885

Mining acquisitions had become commonplace by 1884; larger corporations absorbed Tombstone's smaller mines. The Tombstone Milling & Mining Company purchased the Gilded Age and Way-Up mines for

$23,500, making it one of the largest mining companies in Arizona. In September, they also purchased the Girard's mine and mill property. TMM's manager, George W. Cheyney, advised the *Daily Record Epitaph* that a large group of men was in the process of clearing out the Girard mine so work could begin on it. Cheyney said, "There is no doubt that our properties contain large bodies of ore, which could not be worked at a profit if we were compelled to haul it to the reduction works on the San Pedro, but which can be made to yield a good return with the facilities we now have, by the purchase of the Girard mill."[68] Cheyney advised the reporter the noise of the stamp mills would echo in Tombstone within two to three months.

Mining news from around the nation was important to Tombstone for various reasons. In August, Tombstone papers were filled with information on the latest mining boomtown of Aspen, Colorado. Some residents who feared Tombstone's life was near its end headed for their next hopeful town. Aspen was touted as a place where one could escape the summer heat and avoid the storms of high altitudes.[69] The papers concluded mining strikes were so universal that mining was only a "matter of mathematics in Aspen."

Those involved in the mining business knew the rewards, as well as the dangers. While the investors had money to win or lose, it was the miners who took the real risks. For the paltry wage of four dollars per day, they risked their lives. The dangers of mining were numerous. A miner could drown from rushing underground water, perish from gunpowder explosions, or be burned or scalded with hot water. He also faced injury from wielding an ax while splitting timbers, falls through floors, neck injuries while running up sheaves, falls from the cages or down a shaft. He also had to be aware of the pump compartment, which was filled with projecting iron points and sharp corners. Being a miner was hard work and earned the men the nickname "Toughnut" for working the hard rock.

While the sounds of mining and milling had not been heard in Tombstone for some time, soon many heard those prosperous sounds again. In addition to the Tombstone Milling & Mining Company gearing up again, the mines on Contention Hill were in a race to join them. Their foreman, William Corbett, advised the *Daily Record Epitaph* of their progress. He stated the water in the mines had been lowered by fifty feet, and only thirty-five feet of water was left to be drained. On September 3, 1885, the pump speed was increased from five and one half strokes to seven strokes per minute. Corbett said he first thought it would be three months before the mines were free of water, but because the pumping equipment was working so effectively, he anticipated that it would only take about three weeks. Until the pumping had ceased the previous year, Corbett stated they produced good ore in the five or six winzes that were sunk below the water line.

By late October, progress on Tombstone's mines looked promising. The Grand Central pumps plunged along at a rate of seven to eight strokes per minute, and they had no problem controlling the water. According to foreman Charles Leach, the flow of water into the mine had decreased during the last week. The depth of the main shaft had been increased to eighty-six feet since work on the mine had resumed, and the new shaft was down thirty-one feet below the previous seven-hundred-foot level.

Miners worked four six-hour shifts in the bottom of the shaft, while considerable work was done in various other parts of the mine. Superintendent Gage pushed for development below the water level, but not much progress had been made. Ore was shipped regularly from both the Grand Central and Emerald mines. The daily shipments were about fifty tons from the Grand Central, and about fifteen from the Emerald.[70] Even though ore shipments were good, Gage had to let some miners go from the Emerald mine. He did not anticipate any further layoffs.

The other working mines and mills in town were the Contention works, the Tombstone Milling & Mining Company (TMM) mines, and its Girard mill. Some of the oldest mines in town belonged to TMM and included the Toughnut, Lucky Cuss, West Side, and Girard. TMM's Girard mill, which had been built about four years prior by the Girard company, once again disturbed the silence in Tombstone. The *Daily Record Epitaph*'s reporter wrote, "The mill closed down about three years ago and remained idle until last Tuesday evening when the great engine breathed a sign of relief from its long inactivity, and the great power within it once more asserted itself, the throttle, like the first pulse beat of new life communicated the mighty force to every detail of the complicated machinery which at the instant sprang into a whirl of effective motion and the thunder of the twenty stamps once more greeted many listening ears and cheered regarding the work now in progress."[71]

On November 1, 1885, the mines and mills in Tombstone employed some two hundred men. The various mining companies paid nearly eighteen thousand dollars in one month to miners. Most mines had

Tombstone Mining Co., ore dumping, reproduced by permission of the Arizona Historical Society.

two shifts working the mines. The day shift was from 7:00 a.m. to 6:00 p.m., and the night shift ran from 6:00 p.m. to 3:00 a.m.

Tombstone's mines and mills consumed large amounts of timber, which had to be hauled in from the Huachuca Mountains. It was used for hoists, shafts, and other building needs. Tombstone's monthly consumption of wood at this time was 225 cords per month. Even though ore assayed at $1.50 per ton, the mining company's money was tied up in labor and lumber, so they cut costs wherever they could. The cost of hauling ore to the mill was quite expensive, so the Tombstone Milling & Mining Company came up with a new way to get ore to the mill. In early November they built a fifteen-hundred-foot tramway, which went across the Girard, Toughnut, and Goodenough mines and connected with the tramway for the West Side and Girard mines. The tramway stopped at the hoisting works of the Girard mill, where the ore was crushed.

The year had begun with cold and snowy weather, and hope that the Grand Central pumps, along with the Contention pumps, would extract the water from the mines. They did. The city rumbled from the mighty pumps and the townspeople were exuberant. The mining industry once again appeared stable, and the hum of business and rolling wagons echoed through Tombstone. The people of Tombstone saw their mines working again and expected that by the end of 1886, the previous depression would be no more than a painful memory. Their main fear lay with the demonetizing of silver by President Cleveland and Wall Street.

1886

If the early part of January 1886 was any indication of the rest of the year, then Tombstone's mining prospects looked promising. The Tombstone Milling & Mining Company was doing a large amount of work on the Toughnut, West Side, Girard, Goodenough, Lucky Cuss, and East Side mines. Enough ore had been taken from the West Side mine to keep the mill running for the next two years. The company had about twenty-five thousand tons of manganese ore at their smelter in Charleston. About seventy men kept the smelter running day and night to reduce the ore. The mill at Charleston, however, was not running, so the ore was worked at the Girard mill in Tombstone. The ore was taken from the mine to the mill by cars. The company employed 120 men at the mines and 29 men at the mill with a total of 219 men on the company payroll.

Tragedy struck early in Tombstone that year. A miner was found dead in the shaft of the Silver Plume mine. Miner and musician Tommy Vincent was needed to play at some dances in town and, being too busy to work the mine, he asked Joseph Eisele to work for him. Eisele obliged and went to work at the mine. Since Vincent had not seen Eisele for a couple of days, he went by the mine to see if everything was okay. Unfortunately, it was not. From the appearance of the body, Eisele must have set off a blast that did not go off. Believing it had failed, Eisele bent over the blast, and it exploded, killing him instantly.

Although mining was the lifeblood of many living in the West, residents of the East often failed to recognize it as a legitimate business. According to a *Daily Record Epitaph* story printed on February 25, 1886, most Easterners felt a good piece of property was supposed to pay from the beginning. The article stated, "There is not a more erroneous idea extant in regard to mining than the one that a good property must of necessity from the very start furnish sufficient ore or to not only pay expenses, but also to return dividends to the lucky owners." Mining required a great deal of capital to build housing for employees, and purchase tools and supplies of all kinds. Tunnels had to be driven, shafts sunk, and drifts opened up so the ore could be taken down. Mining moguls in the West were confident financiers in the East would eventually recognize mining as a legitimate and safe business.

Tombstone's weekly mining reviews appeared in the papers, but nothing noteworthy was reported. The mines were operating and extracting ore, but no new finds were discovered. The Vizina mine started hoisting ore again in late February, and at the same time, the smelter in Charleston was taken down and rebuilt in Tombstone. Occasionally, raising ore was delayed because of high wind. This was remedied once the new enclosure was complete. Mining was Tombstone's heart, and many business owners in town often felt its pulse. Dance house owner Pasquale Nigro was one of them. He was now the owner of the Margarita mine. He employed four men to work his mine; and the main shaft was sunk in early March. While sinking the shaft, a large ore body of manganese was discovered.

Tombstone's mining industry started off with a boom and a rush. What was once a bustling mining community was now an average mining town. Tombstone's popularity remained strong until water was discovered in the mines. An immediate reaction was to pack up and leave because, to some, it seemed like the end. However, Tombstone bounced back as pumps were installed to remove the water from the mines. While this action satisfied most, others already had left for new boomtowns with a bright and hopeful future.

Many stayed in Tombstone though, believing the water was a minor setback and that given time and resources, the town would once again shine, as it had in previous years. The March 4, 1886, *Daily Tombstone* paper wrote, "Tombstone is entering upon an era of permanent prosperity. The days of her boom are past forever, but tide of dull times has also passed. A new start has been made."

Many believed ore did not exist below the water level in most mines. However, Tombstone's croakers were convinced when ore bodies were found below water levels in some of Tombstone's largest mines. With that proven, Tombstone once again encouraged hopeful investors to take a risk on Tombstone. Several new developments had been made, mostly in the western end of the district. This new discovery also convinced many of Tombstone's prosperity, because its future wealth was not limited to the original mines that had made Tombstone rich.

Chloriding had become the latest technology used in mining. When using this technique, miners followed a thin vein or discontinuous ore deposit by irregular workings, intent only on extracting the profitable parts, with no regard for development. The term is said to have originated at Silver Reef in southwestern Utah when the rich silver chloride ores were being worked.[72]

With chloriding and regular mining back on track, business owners in town received steady and reliable patronage. Even though their businesses no longer boomed as the mines once had, they experienced a safer and more legitimate business. It appeared Tombstone had reached a solid, conservative level, and its future seemed well fixed.

In March, spring began to peek its head out in Tombstone as the temperature reached sixty-nine degrees and trees started to bud. The *Daily Tombstone* reported, "A little bird whispers that it is a strike of 'capital' in the East, and not a labor strike in San Francisco that delays the work on the Grand Central pumps."[73] It was reported the pumps would work in about three weeks. The *Daily Tombstone* was forced to print its news on brown paper for a few days because its regular paper supply was delayed in getting to town. The Grand Central mine's superintendent, E. B. Gage, his wife, and Josiah White, superintendent of the Contention, all departed Tombstone on March 16, 1886. The Gages were en route to the East for a visit, while White was headed for California.

The Tombstone Milling & Mining Company moved its concentrator from Charleston to Tombstone in mid-March. It was located between the Girard mill and dump. While this company and the Grand Central Company were idle at this time, other mines were worked. Still, the "mining reporter" for the *Daily Tombstone* was not happy with the progress in Tombstone. He wrote a story about the subject and said

Although there is every probability that in the starting of the pumps on the hill, the water question of this district will be finally settled. It seems a one-sided business that two companies should bear the burden and heat of the day whilst those properties adjoining, should take every advantage they can of their ground being drained and not contribute their portion towards maintaining the machinery which pumps the water out. The Tombstone Milling &

Mining Company ought to be one of the biggest contribu-
tors towards a scheme of this sort, but they draw themselves within the warmth of their shell and say, "We have
plenty of ore in sight to keep us running for years, why
should we increase the liabilities of our company for an
object, which we should not receive any benefit from, for
some years if ever."[74]

The reporter also chastised the Empire Company and the Contention
Hill, Mayflower, Way-Up, and Vizina companies for the same thing.

Nonetheless, the mines were being worked. Mr. Corbett of the
Contention said the company had twenty-six men working in various
parts of the mine. They brought up and shipped about twenty tons
daily. In one week, six men raised about one hundred tons of ore,
nearly three tons per man, per day. The Contention mill started again
in late March, after being idle for nearly five months. Because a great
deal of ore had been mined, but not milled, the mill could have been
kept working day and night, if the company chose to operate so.

Mr. Anderson of the Grand Central mine reported carpenters had
been busy at their mine. They were preparing the pump rods with iron
clamps so they would be ready to be placed in the mines. Putting the
pump rods down in the mine, once all pieced together, was not an
easy task. It was estimated it would be late May before the pumps
were ready. There were about twenty miners on a shift, but when you
added the timber men, car men, and others, the Grand Central's payroll showed about eighty men total. The Head Center, Tranquility,
Emerald, Prompter, Ground Hog, and State of Maine mines all
reported similar activity.

A few days after that report, the Tombstone Milling & Mining
Company busily engaged in hiring any and all men for mining. If the
boss on duty could have found more men, they would have been
employed as well. He said, "Every man who wears hair and is practical,
can get work."[75] Some thought this employment rush indicated a
boom for Tombstone in the near future. Because of this, Tombstone's
streets appeared deserted. Large portions of men usually idling
around town were now working in the mines.

On April 2, the new smelter started up, and many of Tombstone's
residents turned out to see their mining community rumble once
more. Just as things looked promising for Tombstone's mining industry, the West Side mine flooded with water. It happened while a winze

was being sunk in the mine, and just after a hole had been drilled and the blast went off. Few were alarmed though, because the pumps would not have a difficult time removing the water.

By mid-April, Tombstone mining companies knew there was a water problem in their mines. However, they felt the future was secure because the water pumps were doing their job. These pumps were, after all, keeping the water out of the mines, allowing quality ore to be extracted. Even the Tombstone Milling & Mining Company said it was saving one thousand dollars monthly by using the extracted water in the Girard mill, rather than paying the Huachuca Water Company. Recent reports from the larger mines reported good progress, but water remained a concern for some residents. They felt eventually the large mining companies would have to pull together and pump out the water jointly, or Tombstone's future might be in jeopardy. The *Daily Tombstone* was supportive of Tombstone's mining future and printed this in its April 8, 1886, issue: "All you croakers that talk about the mines in Tombstone petering out and this camp being dead, just walk one hundred yards from the Occidental Hotel to the Vizina Hoisting Works and gaze on the ore now being taken out daily from said mine."

Tombstone's papers were not the only ones who wrote about its progress. An article appeared in the *Phoenix Herald* about Tombstone's mines and its future. In the optimistic story, the paper described what it was like to go down into the depths of the Grand Central mine. "Go down sir? Step on that cage; hold fast! Six hundred feet! Ready! Down you glide into the darkness of the pit so gently that you scarcely realize at first that you move and then the wind seems to begin to blow up the shaft. Flash! Was that lightning? No. Only the light in the mouth of the 100-foot level. Flash! Another one! One about every two seconds! Gently you glide down now into the glare of the great locomotive headlight at the six hundred foot level, the bottom of the shaft. The great pump cylinders are here and switches and cars and you are in the mouth of a tunnel."[76]

Shortly after that story ran, a rich mining strike was reported at the Tribute mine, owned by the Tombstone Milling & Mining Company. Located just south of the West Side mine, its ledge was reportedly thirty feet and averaging thirty ounces of silver to the ton.

On May 25, 1886, a small fire in town marked the four-year anniversary of Tombstone's second devastating fire. This fire broke out in a "Maison de joie" on Sixth Street between Allen and Fremont.[77]

The fire was quickly subdued with minimal damage done. However, the next day, Tombstone suffered a blow that forever changed its future. When the pumps at the Grand Central had begun working May 15, 1886, and the mine's improvements were reportedly working to the satisfaction of its owners, Tombstone's outlook had appeared good. However, pending negotiations between mining companies left the pumps on the hill idle. On May 26, at 11:00 p.m., the Grand Central hoisting works and pump caught fire and were completely destroyed. The Contention mine was the only one left with any pumps, and it would be a long and costly process before the Grand Central could be back in operation. The pumping machinery had been installed in 1884 at a cost of $175,000. Mining superintendent E. B. Gage was in Boston at the time and, upon hearing the news, headed for Tombstone. The people of Tombstone could only speculate what would become of them and their town. The *Daily Tombstone* wrote, "The people of Tombstone are brave and courageous, and have successfully outlived several drawbacks, and will do so in this case."[78]

Workers first noticed the fire in the engine room and sounded the alarm. Twenty-five men were in the mine when the fire began, and all managed to reach safety. The hoisting works were quickly enveloped in flames, and the wooden supports below fell easy prey to the fire fiend. Smoke rising from the mine the next morning indicated a fire still burned below Tombstone. The fire in the main shaft was put out a couple of days later, and the mine's foreman, Charley Leach, attempted to go down in the mine to assess the damage. Unfortunately, Charley went down in the mine too soon, and he and his men were overpowered by noxious fumes. Upon learning they had not returned, townspeople and miners alike raced to their rescue. Doctors Goodfellow and Willis also hurried to the scene. Thankfully, the men found a safe level and eventually reached the surface. This fire left Tombstone's mining industry idle once more. The heroes of the day were saloonkeeper and miner, Gilbert S. Bradshaw, Charlie and Gus Tribolet, Ike Isaacs, and many others.

Heroes one day, in jail the next—it seemed the Tribolet brothers had their share of problems when it came to alcohol. This time it was brother Godfrey, who was accused of selling liquor without a license and smuggling mescal across the border. Godfrey was released on the charge of selling liquor without a license because the jury disagreed. However, promptly after his release he was rearrested for smuggling mescal liquor over the border. He was taken before the U.S. Court Commissioner, who held Tribolet over until October for a grand jury appearance. If convicted, he faced a jail sentence of three to five years and a fine from three to five thousand dollars or both. Meanwhile, his brother Charlie was released on his arrest for selling liquor without a license. Legal problems aside, Charlie was later nominated as chief engineer of the Tombstone Fire Department.

Superintendent Gage quickly reached Tombstone a few days after the Grand Central fire. While he waited to meet with an appraiser from his insurance company, it was determined a new shaft could be started within ten days. Meanwhile, foreman Charley Leach was finally able to determine some facts about the fire. He knew it was still not safe to enter the mine and ascertained it had caved in and filled the shaft up to about twenty feet from the opening.

Progress on the new shaft was swift, but when shift boss McCloud tried to connect to the Grand Central's old shaft, fumes permeated. After a much-awaited meeting between mine owners and insurance appraisers, the insurance company agreed to pay the fully insured amount of eighty-five thousand dollars. The *Daily Tombstone* interviewed Superintendent Gage about the Grand Central's situation. He was reportedly very positive in his tone, but advised the paper no efforts would be made until the new shaft reached the main shaft. Once the damage was assessed, they would proceed. He did say, however, that if no damage existed below the three-hundred-foot level, it was believed the existing shaft could be repaired.

As if mining problems in Tombstone weren't bad enough, Apache raids on local ranches made Tombstone residents nervous. Every day the papers were filled with news of Indian raids, scalpings, and burned ranches. Tombstone residents didn't fear all Indians though. Despite raiding Apaches, friendly Papago Indians were frequently seen on Tombstone's streets. The Apache situation became so bad that the newspapers started carrying full columns of notices and pleas to the governor and the president of the United States. Mine pumps burning, and Indian depredations aside, the value of silver was fast becoming a major concern to Tombstone's residents and investors. People in Tombstone blamed speculators in Europe and the United States for the falling silver prices.

In late July, silver was worth ninety-seven cents. However, by early August, the price had dropped to ninety-one cents. It was this price-dropping trend that caused the Tombstone Milling & Mining Company

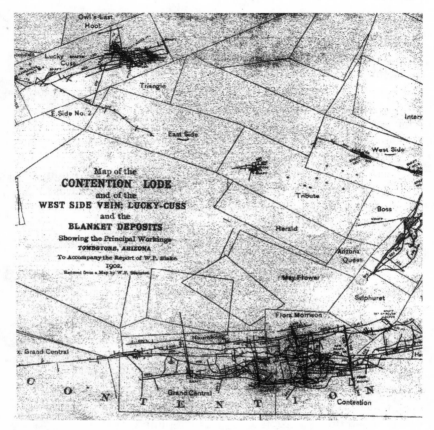

Mining map, Grand Central mines, from the author's collection.

to shut down their operations for good on August 16, 1886. Mr. George Cheyney, the company's manager, notified the newspaper of the decision. Cheyney did say, however, that if the price of silver rose again, enough for the company to make money, mining would resume. The company discharged its miners, but before doing so, paid their wages in full. The Tombstone Milling & Mining Company had been a strong force in Tombstone for many years, even after the miners' strike in 1884. From October 1884 until July 1, 1886, the company mined and milled 27,875 tons of ore. From that, silver and gold bullion was produced at a value of $508,144.45. During that same period, the furnace produced base bullion yielding silver, gold, and lead worth $505,187.71. Combined, the company made $1,103,017.77.

Thinking the end was at hand, the people of Tombstone were excited to hear reports from the company indicating it might be having second thoughts about closing operations completely down. Even as the Tombstone Milling & Mining Company was shutting down, the Grand Central mill was being rebuilt after the fire. A new building on its site was to open and be used as a concentrating room.

As Tombstone's future loomed in the balance, a couple of spirited poker games took place, the price of silver held at ninety-five cents, and rich ore was constantly hoisted from the Vizina mine. Tombstone's founder, Ed Schieffelin, was now in California. Ed left Tombstone shortly after discovering the mines and amassing large amounts of cash. Since Ed was a prospector, it was more of a thrill to find the silver than to settle down with it. Ed's latest prospecting journey led him to San Bernardino, where he was in search of his next strike.

Tombstone started feeling a little better about its future when the price of silver reached ninety-nine cents on October 28, 1886, and one dollar in early November. Not able to hold its literary tongue any longer, the *Daily Tombstone* published a story about the rise in silver prices. The paper pointed out that the major mining companies had closed down in Tombstone because of the falling silver prices. Since that time, silver had steadily risen in price; however, they had not reopened the mines. They advised all those miners chloriding the mines to keep doing so, because all their hard work would pay off with the rising silver prices. The *Daily Tombstone* also noted several prominent mine owners were in Tombstone in early November, and claimed that it looked as if something important were on the tapis. It was around this time when machinery and new hoisting works were set up at the Lucky Cuss mine. Once in place, the hiss of steam was heard. Shortly thereafter, ore was brought up from below Tombstone's belly.

By December, silver had risen to $1.02, but the larger mines remained idle. The mines did resume operations for a while during the early part of 1887, but by April, the price of silver dropped to ninety-four cents. It was just a matter of time before Tombstone's population hit its lowest point. The 1900 census revealed only 646 hardy souls remained in town. These were largely supported by county courthouse activities.

Chapter Two

A Hearty Welcome

Tombstone's Saloons

Once Tombstone's mining boom had begun, savvy entrepreneurs wasted no time in setting up their businesses. Saloon operators followed the mining circuit and quickly appeared at potential boomtowns. One of Tombstone's first saloons, which opened to support the mines, was a little place called Danner & Owens saloon. It had opened by late 1878 and was located on Tombstone's first townsite near the West Side Mine.

1879

On March 5, 1879, a new townsite had been established and businesses moved to the new location. By mid-1879, Charles Brown, who offered weary travelers a good meal, opened the camp's first restaurant. The Calhoun brothers opened the Pioneer Saloon, thought to be this site's first, and supplied spirituous liquids. Thomas Corrigan also started a saloon. John Montgomery and Edward Benson had opened the famed O.K. Corral on Third Street earlier in the year. The first house to be built in Tombstone was erected in June by James B. "Pie" Allen. His building was located at the corner of Fourth and Allen Streets and was used as a store. The U.S. Postal Department named Richard Gird postmaster general in December 1878, and Michael Gray was appointed justice of the peace. With all this and more, the camp was thought to be established with life and spirit.[1]

Supplies were also shipped to Tombstone from Tucson through freighters and stages. Some of the big suppliers in Tucson shipped

THE DISCOVERY OF AMERICA.

Ayers sarsaparilla ad no. 1, from the author's collection.

orders to authorized agents representing them in Tombstone, like wholesale liquor dealer Henry G. Horton. Horton offered his new Tombstone customers liquors, cigars, whiskey, brandy, rum, and a variety of wines. Many Tucson merchants eventually left for the more promising Tombstone. Another Tucson beverage merchant who sold to Tombstone was J. F. Innis. His nonspirituous beverages complemented the spirituous ones sold by Horton, and included sarsaparilla, ginger ale, bar syrups, and champagne cider.

On August 20, 1879, Sylvester Comstock and Fielding C. Brown established a saloon called the Mount Hood on Allen Street. They purchased lot six in block four on Allen Street for $250 from Charles Calhoun, one of Tombstone's citizens who laid out the 320-acre plat where Tombstone sits. Their large tent saloon quickly became one of Tombstone's favorites. In a place where work was hard and women were few, saloons were a haven for lonely miners. Tombstone began to see a large number of saloons open rapidly.

John "Jack" Doling opened his "dispensary" on Allen Street. Oddly enough, he advertised that it was on Main Street, but since Allen was the "main" street, Doling was correct. However, it could have been misleading for someone wandering the camp looking for Main Street. His ad stated, "Call frequently. Drink moderately. Pay on delivery. Take your departure quietly."

Henry Fry was also in the beverage business and offered choice liquors and cigars at his place on Allen. Fry, however, lost his business in 1884 for defaulting on a note. Randall and Horner had a

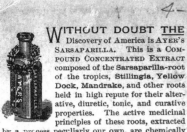

Ayers sarsaparilla ad no. 2, from the author's collection.

saloon, too, but additionally offered the recreational sport of billiards. Jim Vizina and Benjamin Cook added their names to the already long list of saloon owners. They poured alcohol, sold cigars, and claimed, "Visitors made to feel at home by the hospitality of 'Jim' and 'Ben.' Happiness for the jovial, and a shady bower for rest and recuperation."

Benjamin Cook was born in Beverly, Massachusetts, in 1832, and the nearby Atlantic Ocean was his backyard. It had tempted many a young man, including Cook, to join seafaring life at an early age. By nineteen, Ben had reached California, where he gave up the sea for mining and prospecting. His quest for mineral wealth led him to Idaho, British Columbia, and eventually Arizona, where he found his fortune in Tombstone.

Jim and Ben welcomed exhausted stagecoach passengers who made the fourteen-hour journey to their lively town. In the fall, J. D. Kinnear began operating a stage line between Tucson and Tombstone.

He made semiweekly trips until the demand grew and he increased his runs to three times a week. In December, a much-needed second stage line was started by H. C. Walker & Company. Since Walker offered daily trips between cities, J. D. Kinnear increased his trips to match the competition's.

1880

When hopeful arrivals reached Tombstone in early 1880, they were greeted with an array of businesses to make their lives more comfortable. Pioneer business owners welcomed them, competing for their attention. Many of the first people who started businesses in Tombstone followed the mining or gambling circuit. Tombstone was just the next stop along the way to their next big strike. Colonel Fielding C. Brown, of the Mount Hood Saloon, was one of those individuals. Brown was quoted as saying, "A hearty welcome for everyone, be he forty-niner or 'tenderfoot.'"[2] Former Tucson residents also flocked to booming Tombstone. James Vogan, who previously operated a saloon in Tucson, along with James Flynn, started a saloon on Allen Street.

Liquor distributors, like Colonel Roderick F. Hafford, also sold tobacco. Hafford opened his business on April 12, 1880, on Allen Street. It was nestled between two of Tombstone's biggest hotels—the Cosmopolitan and Brown's. While not a wholesale business, the glorious Cosmopolitan Hotel had a saloon for its guests. Aptly named the Cosmopolitan Saloon, it was run by William T. Knapp and "Buckskin" Frank Leslie.

Most wholesale liquor dealers purchased their supplies from Tucson and San Francisco merchants and directly from Kentucky distributors. Edward Roberts was a liquor distributor in town but kept no bar and sold only by measure from the keg or barrel. His wine supply was from a Los Angeles, California, manufacturer and his liquor remained in its original casks and barrels.

Many residents had a strong connection to California since many early Tombstonians either hailed from California or had last resided there. California also served as the summer home for many who wished, and could afford, to escape the Arizona summer heat. Many Tombstone businesses were closely connected to California as well. They were either named after popular California businesses, offered prime California commodities, or were named after California towns.

Tombstone rapidly became home to many hardworking people. When these people were done with their daily duties, they needed a

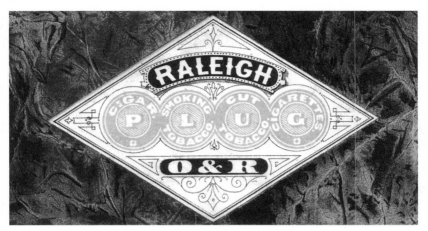

Old Raleigh tobacco ad, from the author's collection.

place to unwind. Some unwound at home with their families, while others "mellowed" in town. There were plenty of places for one to relax after a hard day's work, such as the Tombstone Headquarters, run by John J. Inwall, who was the sole agent for the Philadelphia Brewery of Los Angeles. In one week alone, he disposed of one hundred kegs of the lager. Inwall advertised "a favorite place of resort for all those who are lovers of a delightful beverage." He kept on hand all kinds of liquors and ales, as well as cigars. His saloon also had a private room for gentlemen, and kept all the California newspapers on file. His advertisement also stated, "All Sacramentans registered here." His saloon was noted for the eighty-by-twelve-foot painting of a ship on canvas, which adorned the saloon's wall.

A. O. Wallace and J. M. Clark ran the San Diego Keg House, which was a popular saloon in Tombstone with a California connection. They advertised they were the sole agents for the "celebrated Thistle Dew Whiskey." The Alhambra was another popular saloon in town; it was named after a California resort. Well established by early June 1880, and run by Thomas Corrigan, the saloon was located on Allen Street, next to the Golden Eagle Brewery. The Alhambra measured thirty by eighty feet; the front contained the saloon, while the rear housed the clubrooms. Usually six to eight banking games, such as faro, were played nightly. The *Nugget* described this saloon as "the boss place as a favorite resort and magnificent resort and has no superior outside San Francisco." The Alhambra's crowning feature was the bar and its

Old Reliable cigar ad, from
the author's collection.

fixtures, which were said to have been superb pieces of workmanship.
In the center of the saloon sat a large Gothic chair with velvet and
Morocco upholstery in which the "ruling spirit sat on his throne to
watch over" his saloon. On both sides were bar fixtures made of walnut, mahogany, and rosewood. They were adorned with wrought and
filigree work, neatly gilded and finished. The drinking glasses were
extravagant sets of Bohemian, Italian, and French ware of splendid
designs and patterns. The bar stock was expansive and included the
finest drinks, the best liquor, the choicest imported wines, brandies,
liquors, and cigars. The *Nugget* said, "The mass of people . . . can support anything that is truly bon ton and tony."[3] Mr. Corrigan had other
interests in Tombstone and owned several mines, including the
Bradshaw, the Lily, and the Washington.

Corrigan was a partner in the Dauntless mine with John H.
Honison, but sometimes owning a mine became a problem. Corrigan
and Honison purchased the mine from a group of men, including C. M.
Grattan, for six thousand dollars. Once this transaction came to light,
another man, H. O. Weller, filed a judgment against Grattan, and his
partner, along with Corrigan and Honison in May 1880. He claimed he
was given no compensation for the sale of the mine and that Corrigan
and Honison never paid for it. Weller told the court that he and
Grattan had established a partnership in 1879 and when Grattan and
his other partners located the Dauntless mine, he was still Grattan's
partner. He therefore asked the court to recognize his partnership with
C. M. Grattan, give him one half interest in the mine, and establish a
trust in his favor with his share of funds from the mine. The outcome
of that judgment is unknown.

By June 1880, Tombstone had approximately sixteen saloons, including the Diana Lodging House and Saloon, previously known as the Evening Star Saloon. The saloon of proprietors Miles Kellogg and Mr. Morris was at 316 Allen, below Fourth Street. They refitted the old building and furnished it as a lodging house with a saloon in the front. Kellogg and his band also performed for local balls and social parties. A year later, Kellogg was found guilty of keeping a disorderly house.[4]

Another one of Tombstone's saloons was the ever-popular Palace Saloon and billiard hall. This saloon, first owned by William T. Lowery and Robert H. Archer, was adorned with elegant furnishings and paintings and welcomed weary workers to play billiards and enjoy the clubrooms. By July though, Lowery was no longer involved with the saloon, and Archer had taken on a man named Campbell as his partner. The Palace Saloon also acquired a new specimen of copper, which was proudly displayed in the saloon. The copper was taken from the rapidly growing Copper Queen Mine in Bisbee. About a month after the Palace's opening, a fire ignited in the back of the saloon, but it was quickly extinguished. It seems a cauldron of tar left over from recent renovations to the saloon was accidentally ignited. However, thanks to quick response, no damage was sustained.

Whiskey and tobacco were usually enjoyed together in mining towns like Tombstone. By mid-June 1880, Tombstone residents could buy cigarettes, tobacco, and cigars just about anywhere. Saloons, gambling halls, stationery stores, and mercantile stores all featured tobacco products. William A. Bourland had a small shop on Fifth Street where he sold cigars, tobacco, pipes, and stationery. Bourland advertised "Genuine Durham, Seal of North Carolina, Old Judge, and Vanity Fair Tobacco." He also received a large consignment of cigars from San Francisco, which he offered at $3.50 to $13.00 per hundred, in a box.

Joseph Goldtree & Co. opened a large shop on Allen Street and sold notions, fancy goods, perfume, stationery, tobacco, and cigars. The store's manager, Albert Fortlouis, advertised "Smoke Ganymede cigars, 2 for 25 cents," and "Chew Out of the Sea tobacco." Goldtree's store also housed a circulating library; the first of its kind in Tombstone, it offered some 250 volumes of reading material.

Despite its name, Kelly's Wine House sold more than claret and Chardonnay. Julius A. Kelly, a newcomer to town, opened his wine house on Fremont Street, just one door from Fourth Street. It was a splendid, beautifully decorated, adobe building. Mr. Kelly sold wholesale and

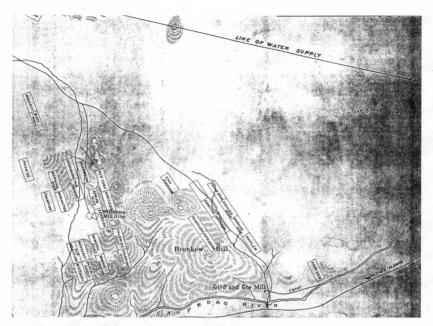

Bronkow Hill mining map, April 1879, courtesy of the Arizona
Historical Society.

retail wines, liquors, and cigars. His wine house also contained three
billiard tables. A month after opening, Kelly proudly exhibited a new
sample of ore from the old Bronkow mine, in which he was a partner.
However, Kelly shortly thereafter withdrew his claim to any interest in
the Bronkow mine, which was now known as the Dean Richmond mine.
On August 2, 1880, Kelly opened a "branch bit" saloon on Allen Street. He
offered an immense lunch to his patrons at this location, along with
seven-year-old Muscat angelica wine and six-year-old Kentucky apple
brandy. His newest addition, located just two doors down from Wells,
Fargo & Co.'s office, was in Heitzleman's building. In early September, he
sold his old wine house on Fremont Street to Valentine Mand. Mand,
who had come from Los Angeles, promised to maintain Kelly's old business, along with its reputation. Kelly's Wine House also served as a meeting place for Tombstone's Republicans. A notice was placed in the paper
advising all Republicans in town, as well as in nearby vicinities, to meet
at Kelly's to form a club and take other action that would benefit the
party. Two years later, Julius A. Kelly became secretary of the Tombstone
Republican Party.

The summer of 1880 found Tombstone's business population exploding. There were twelve general merchandise stores, four hotels, nine restaurants, five corrals, several lawyers, four lumberyards, two breweries, ten cigar stores, two furniture stores, two banks, five assay offices, and several saloons. Tombstone's human population was also exploding, and reached some three thousand inhabitants according to the latest census.[5] Taking the census proved to be a difficult task for Philip M. Thurmond, mainly because of the miners. If they weren't working underground in the mines, they were usually sleeping during the day. To ensure the most accurate results, Thurmond set up a table in Comstock & Brown's, from three o'clock to six o'clock, and eight o'clock until eleven o'clock, to accommodate the miners' shifts. Comstock & Brown announced their tent saloon was about to be replaced with a new two-story structure. The tent, which they had placed at the rear of the lot while construction was completed, was removed. The new saloon was attached to the Grand Hotel. Setting up a census table in a saloon was not a problem, since most stayed open all the time. Arizona pioneer, Mrs. Hempe, knew of Tombstone's history and later wrote, "Saloons and gambling places were always open, in fact the town never slept, it was full of life from day-break to day-break, and then some—a beehive of activity."[6]

In addition to saloons, Tombstone had its own breweries. The Golden Eagle Brewery, owned by Bernhardt Wehrfritz and Sigfried Tribolet, was Tombstone's first. The brewery was located on the corner of Fifth and Allen Streets, in the heart of everything. The front of the building was used as a saloon, while the stone building in the back, equal in size, was used for making and storing beer. The brewery's capacity was twenty-five kegs per day. The brewery sold its beer at $7.50 for a ten-gallon keg, $3.75 for a five-gallon keg, or three bottles for one dollar. The saloon also contained a reading room, where patrons ordered fresh brewed beer or selected from a variety of imported goods, including cigars. Wehrfritz was left to run this popular business by himself for about a month when his partner, Sigfried, left town to get married. Sigfried traveled to his sweetheart's hometown of Dubuque, Iowa, where they exchanged marriage vows.

To help keep their products cool and refreshing, Tombstone brewers and saloon owners, as well as other business owners, relied on ice. Despite its lack of readily available water, Tombstone's atmosphere was about to be enhanced by an ice factory. An ice factory meant more ice, at cheaper prices, and restaurants, housekeepers, hotels, and especially saloons, welcomed this new business. Until that time however, Tombstone businesses would have to continue to rely on ice that was delivered to town by the Tombstone Stage Line, run by Ed Swift. His company was an agent for Paul Moroney's Ice Company of Tucson, which sold ice to Tombstone's residents. Moroney was the first to introduce ice to Tucson, and then Tombstone. He began his business by making a deal with the railroad company, who used Truckee, California, ice to accommodate railroad employees and passenger trains. Moroney obtained permission from the railroad company to sell ice exclusively to the public. However, Tombstone's reliance on imported ice would soon end. The *Arizona Daily Star* printed an article from the July 4 issue of Tombstone's *Nugget* regarding the plans for an ice factory near Tombstone. The article stated several individuals announced their idea of establishing an ice factory in the district. The site they chose was near Charleston, which was considered the most centrally located town for the ice shipments. They were so confident their ice factory would be built that they already had five-ton capacity ice machines shipped to them. They also stated they intended to sell the ice at reasonable rates, so everyone could afford it.

It was a hot summer day in 1880 when Clara Spaulding Brown arrived in this "peaceable community." Clara was the wife of mining speculator Theodore Brown, who had been living in Tombstone since 1879. He, like others, believed Tombstone was promising, so he sent for Clara. Clara was no ordinary Victorian housewife, and once she arrived in Tombstone, she became involved in church activities and local theatrical performances. During her stay in Tombstone, Clara acted as the *San Diego Union*'s correspondent. She wrote several letters back to her hometown paper and kept Californians up to date on Tombstone's progress.

She wrote her first letter on July 7, 1880. In it, she described her journey east to Tombstone. Clara talked about the blazing heat she encountered in Yuma, Arizona, and the rough waters of the Colorado River. She was glad to have reached Tucson, where she slept in a bed for the first time since leaving California. The last phase of her trip was the stagecoach ride to Tombstone. Clara wrote, "The dreaded stage ride proved quite enjoyable, for a comfortable Concord coach with six fresh horses, no jam and jolly companions, tended to comfort and light spirits. We arrived at the stage office just back of the town. It is a place of more pretension than I had imagined, and full of activity, notwithstanding the hundreds of loungers seen upon the streets. The only attractive places visible are the liquor and gambling saloons, which are everywhere present, and are carpeted and comfortably furnished. The ladies of Tombstone are not so liberally provided with entertainment and find little enjoyment aside from a stroll about town after sunset, the only comfortable time of the day. The camp is one of the dirtiest places in the world. When black garments appear to have been laid away in an ash barrel, and one is never sure of having a clean face, despite repeated ablutions, it is time to talk about dirt. The soil lies loose upon the surface, and is whirled into the air every day by a wind which almost amounts to a gale; it makes the eyes smart like the cinders from an engine; it penetrates into the houses, and covers everything with dust. I do not believe the famous Nebraska breeze can go ahead of the Tombstone zephyr."[7]

Excitement was something Tombstone never seemed short on, especially in the saloon business. July 19, 1880, proved to be a memorable night for many, when a rather inebriated man sat in a saloon, tempting fate. He delicately placed a live tarantula in his mouth. He repeated his experiment several times, without being bit. The *Epitaph* claimed, "Instinct probably teaching the reptile that preservation is the first law of nature, and to bite him was certain death." Another incident, at the Mount Hood Saloon, resulted in a rather painful ending. One of the saloon's proprietors, Colonel Fielding Brown, was opening a wine bottle when the corkscrew slipped and entered his right hand. The colonel recovered and continued to serve at his post at the bar.

It was during this time when pioneer saloon men James Vizina and Ben Cook completed their block of rental stores at the corner of Fifth and Allen. They leased the corner store for $560 to Milton Joyce who eventually opened a saloon. The *Nugget* announced that by the end of July, Joyce would open an elegantly and elaborately furnished saloon, known as the Oriental. The center building was leased to Charles Glover & Co., who opened a gentlemen's furnishing store, and the third store was rented to the dry goods firm known as L. Myers & Co.

The Oriental Saloon, owned by Milton Joyce & Co., opened its doors on July 21, 1880. The *Epitaph* reported this "soon to be famous" saloon was the most elegantly furnished saloon "this side of the Golden Gate." The *Epitaph* reporter gave a detailed description of the saloon.

> Twenty-eight burners suspended in neat chandeliers
> afforded an illumination of ample brilliancy, and the
> bright rays reflected from many colored crystals on the bar
> sparkled like a December iceling in the sunshine. The
> saloon comprised two apartments. To the right of the main
> entrance is the bar, beautifully carved, finished in white
> gilt and capped with a handsomely polished top. In the
> rear of this stand a brace of side-boards which are simply
> elegant and must be seen to be appreciated. They were
> made for the Baldwin Hotel, of San Francisco, but being
> too small, Mr. Joyce purchased them. The back apartment
> is covered with brilliant Brussels carpet, and suitably fur-
> nished after the style of a grand club room, with conven-
> iences for the wily dealers in polished ivory. The selection
> of furniture and fixtures displays an exquisite taste, and
> nothing seems to have been forgotten—even a handsome
> stock of stationery.[8]

Presiding over the bar was Johnny Chenowith, a brother of the famous pedestrian. Walking matches were very popular during this time, and Chenowith's brother was obviously a champion in the field as referenced in the newspaper story. Chenowith didn't just pour Rock and Rye whiskey into a glass; he created wonderful specialty drinks like Brandy Smashes, A. V. H. Gin, and Russian Cocktails. The *Epitaph* reported, "If he can set up drinks as fast as his brother can score at a walking match, he will be an invaluable treasure to his employers."[9] The Oriental even attracted the Tombstone Glee Club, which began rehearsing there in late July. Two months later, patrons were serenaded by pianist Charley Willoughby, while former Tucson caterer Isaac "Little Jakey" Jacobs provided patrons with delicious morsels. Jacobs provided the Oriental's customers with fresh oysters, shrimp, and crabs imported from San Francisco.

It didn't matter which saloon or which town one visited when it came to labeling a drunk. According to an article in the Tombstone, Arizona's *Daily Nugget*, different parts of the country had various sayings for being drunk and disorderly. In Gotham the drunk was "on a tear," in Chicago he was "on a hoorah," and in Kansas City he was "ginned up for all that's out." In Leadville "the galoot's on a roarer again," in Virginia City he was "on a toot," in Benson he was

Tombstone Saloon, 1880s, reproduced by permission of the Arizona Historical Society.

"pressing his tansy," and in Tombstone no one ever got drunk, although a fellow occasionally made "a holy show of himself."[10]

While it's true that wine, beer, and whiskey were largely consumed in most Western saloons, many offered fancy mixed drinks. They were quite popular in the wealthier communities, like San Francisco, Denver, and Tombstone. Even though this list appeared in 1881, these drinks were popular throughout the 1880s. Fifteen of the most popular drinks in 1881 were:

1. Whiskey cocktails
2. Gin slings
3. Mint juleps
4. Toddies, sweet, sour, and plain
5. Whiskey punch
6. Claret sangaree
7. Apple jack
8. Eggnog
9. Tom & Jerry
10. Sweet potato brandy
11. Ginger pop
12. Root beer

13. Stone fence
14. Hub punch
15. Lemonade—with a stick.[11]

Newcomer Clara Brown wrote, "Saloon openings are all the rage. The Oriental is simply gorgeous and is pronounced the finest place of the kind this side of San Francisco. The bar is a marvel of beauty; the sideboards were made for the Baldwin Hotel; the gaming room connected is carpeted with Brussels; brilliantly lighted, and furnished with reading matter and writing materials for its patrons. Every evening music from the piano and violin attracts a crowd; and the scene is really a gay one—but for all the men. To be sure, there are frequent dances, which I have heard called, 'respectable,' but so long as so many members of the demi-monder who are numerous and very showy here patronize them, many honest women will hesitate to attend."[12–14]

One of the dance houses Clara referred to was the Comet Saloon, owned by Pasquale Nigro. Most dance houses were found above and below the center of town and provided female companionship or "hostesses" for their male patrons. Because competition was tough, each business needed an edge. Nigro provided his customers with music and hired a brass band to entertain patrons at his dance house. Residents residing in upper Tombstone were also treated to the melodies, which poured into the streets.

While some people, like Clara Brown, frowned on Tombstone's dance houses, the town's treasury felt just the opposite. One dance house on Fifth Street announced its reopening in early September. The *Epitaph* noted, "Lovers of the light fantastic are given an opportunity to once again indulge in the pleasure attendant upon the staid quadrille or lively waltz. We are glad to see it going also, as every night's license adds five dollars to the fund for keeping Tombstone's streets in good order."[15]

The Dragoon Saloon was featured in the newspaper again, but this time, it was not because of its creative advertising. It seems a man was sitting on the porch of the saloon discussing palmistry with a friend, when Apache Louise suddenly interrupted his dissertation. She was one of Tombstone's *less refined* women, and approached him from behind, threw her arms around his neck, and began calling him pet names in seven different languages. Tombstone continued to be a town that surprised no one.

Gin bottles illustration, *Harry Johnson's Bartender's Guide*, 1882, from the author's collection.

T. J. Waters was considered a sporting man about town. He was about forty years old, over six feet tall, and weighed in around 190 pounds. When sober, he was also referred to as a clever sort of man. However, after visiting some of his favorite mixologists, Waters became easily irritated. After winning a considerable amount of money gambling in the saloons, he decided to celebrate. He even bought himself a new black and blue plaid shirt, little realizing his modest purchase would cost him dearly. Waters proudly sported his new shirt around town, but received quite a ribbing as he strolled Tombstone's streets. After more than his share of alcohol, Waters failed to find humor in his shirt any longer. He began to grow angry and abusive, announcing, "Now if anyone don't like what I've said let him get up, G-d d—n him. I'm chief. I'm boss. I'll knock the first s— of a b—— down that says anything about my shirt again." Waters had just finished his statement, in the back of Tom Corrigan's Alhambra Saloon, when his good friend and partner Edward L. Bradshaw walked in. Unaware of Waters's warning, Bradshaw made some unpleasant remark about Waters's shirt. Without a word, Waters punched Bradshaw in the left eye, sending him unconscious to the floor. Waters then walked over to Vogan & Flynn's saloon to see, as he said, "If any s— of a b—— there didn't like his shirt." After that, Waters returned to Corrigan's saloon. Before Waters arrived though, Bradshaw had regained his composure, gone back to his cabin to bandage his eye, and put a pistol in his pocket. He came back to Allen Street and took his usual seat in front of Vogan & Flynn's saloon. Bradshaw saw Waters in Corrigan's doorway and crossed the street toward the Golden Eagle Brewery. Meeting Waters, Bradshaw asked, "Why did you do that?"[16] Waters replied, whereupon Bradshaw drew his pistol and fired four shots, all hitting Waters, who died shortly thereafter. Tombstone's law officers promptly arrested Bradshaw. On July 28, Judge Gray denied Bradshaw bail and he was remanded to the Pima County sheriff's office until the grand jury convened in Tucson in September. Bradshaw was eventually found not guilty. Incidentally, the July 29, 1880, *Daily Epitaph* announced that Wyatt Earp had been appointed as deputy sheriff of Pima County, reporting to Charles Shibell. The *Epitaph* wrote, "Wyatt has filled various positions in which bravery and determination were requisites, and in every instance proved himself the right man in the right place." Upon accepting this appointment, Wyatt resigned his post as Wells, Fargo & Co. shotgun messenger, and his brother Morgan succeeded him.

Saloons were big business in most mining communities, and Tombstone had its share of them, from small, basic drinking houses, to large elaborate establishments. The Criterion Saloon and Chop House was a moderate drinking establishment in town. Located at the upper end of Allen, it was owned by Arthur Britton and Gus Lee. Lee had recently bought into the business after Britton and Williams dissolved their partnership. Britton and Lee kept their refreshment stand open day and night for those in need of refreshing. Unfortunately, the Criterion was closed by attachment on July 29, 1880, since Arthur Britton skipped out with the assets. He left Gus Lee, his unfortunate partner, to face the music. Gus eventually found employment at the Occidental Saloon and then later became its owner.

A popular tent saloon in Tombstone was Otto Esch's Park Brewery Depot on Allen Street. Esch and his partner Bernhard "Ben" Hotz were the sole distributors for Levin's Brewery in Tucson. Even though Levin's beer was the house specialty, Otto and Ben kept a full selection of liquors, wines, and cigars on hand. Like many, Otto and Ben knew each other before coming to Tombstone. They first met in Denver in

1873, and then knew each other in California. On May 31, saloon owner Charles Rodig filed a complaint against Otto and his partner. Rodig claimed they ousted and ejected him from his Allen Street premises, which cost him two hundred dollars in losses.

A couple of months later, while the case was pending, Otto returned to his native Disburg, Rheinish, Prussia, for a family visit. According to the *Epitaph*, while he was there, he contracted a fever he could not shake. He made it to Los Angeles, where he rested so he could make it back to Tombstone. He arrived in Tombstone on the thirteenth and was immediately put under the care of Dr. Edward Seely. Unfortunately, Otto passed away on August 14, 1880.

Rodig's case against Esch and Hotz never went to court, according to attorney William Hunsaker, who advised the case should be dismissed as it was settled. Hotz was Esch's sole heir, so he sold the saloon business to Rodig for eight hundred dollars. The paper reported that on August 25 Rodig had already erected a sixteen-by-thirty-foot building on Allen Street next to Otto Geisenhofer's bakery.

Esch's parents and only sister had passed away. He and Hotz were said to be very close friends. So close, that Hotz was at Otto's side when he died. In an affidavit, Hotz stated Otto had some small goods in San Francisco and some property in his native land, but did not know its value. He also said Otto returned from the old country with about one thousand dollars.

The coroner's office performed an autopsy and stated Otto had died showing all the signs of poisoning. Tombstone attorney Thomas J. Drum filed Esch's will with the court shortly after he died, and it appeared everything was "cut and dry." However, as time went on, a mysterious letter was sent to the probate judge. The writer claimed Esch's death was no accident, and the guilty party appeared to be Bernhard Hotz. The writer stated Esch had returned to Tombstone from his native land with a large inheritance. The inheritance was said to have been about twenty thousand dollars, and was in addition to the money Hotz said Esch had.[17] Because of the rumors circulating in town about Hotz, he had Esch's stomach sent to a well-known analytical chemist in San Francisco. The chemist examined the stomach and on September 29 wrote, "After careful research, I have failed to find any poison in the stomach of Otto Esch."[18] On October 14, 1880, Hotz petitioned the court to settle the estate. The outcome is unknown.

Believe it or not, Tombstone business owners had to deal with Internal Revenue collectors. According to the Internal Revenue law,

IRS liquor stamp for special tax, 1880, from the author's collection.

they were required to have a license, whether it be for a brewery, a saloon, or selling tobacco. The licenses were annual, but needed to be punched for each month they were used. Internal Revenue collector Cordis named attorney Wells Spicer as Tombstone's revenue officer. Spicer was supplied with the necessary blank forms, and business owners were urged to get their forms as soon as possible to avoid severe penalties.

One man applying for a new revenue license was Thomas Corrigan. On September 11, 1880, Corrigan reopened his Alhambra Saloon. Despite its grand opening just a few months earlier, the new Alhambra was a sight to behold. The first thing patrons witnessed was the new bar made of black walnut, handsomely embossed in gold. Behind the bar were two elegant sideboards of walnut, mounted with bird's-eye maple. A glittering array of decanters and glasses standing on the bar was said to be a scene of artistic beauty. The bartenders, Andy Robertson and L. A. Geary, always pleasant and smiling, eagerly stood behind the bar waiting to serve thirsty customers. The walls of the bar and reading room were tastefully covered with elegant paintings and engravings of the great masters. The Alhambra's chandeliers were made of bronze and gold. The *Epitaph* reported that the chandeliers, "when lit cast such a flood of dazzling light over the surroundings as to lead to the impression that Aladdin's cave had been rediscovered and we were in the midst of it."[19] Corrigan had also raised the ceiling of his saloon and covered the walls with an elegant Victorian paper of the time.

At the grand reopening Corrigan provided a three-piece orchestra, which played the latest and most fashionable music. The Alhambra's three gambling tables were surrounded by crowds of gamblers eager to tempt "the fickle goddess." About a month before its grand reopening, a row over a poker game had taken place between two gamblers. Pistols were drawn, but interference was rendered, and the squabble ended without bloodshed.

According to the Tombstone newspapers, the Alhambra's reopening was a noted event. The *Epitaph* remarked, "Tom's good-natured face can be seen as he greets with a friendly handshake some old-time friends. The stock of liquors and cigars cannot be excelled in Arizona. Everything in this line has been procured regardless of expense and with an eye...to the taste of his numerous patrons. The reopening was in every sense a grand success and argues well for the Alhambra again resuming the place it occupied prior to Tom's visit East."[20] Shortly after reopening his saloon, Tom left Tombstone yet again, this time for San Francisco. He returned from his visit a month later, on October 19, 1880.

Down the street from Tom's Alhambra was Marshall Williams's cigar stand. It stood in the Wells, Fargo & Co. office and supplied residents with a variety of smoking products. His cigar supply included Key West, Owl, Club House, Española, Plantation, and Hespero brands, as well as playing cards, including squared and un-squared faro cards. For those who preferred cigarettes, he offered Bull Durham, World's Fair, and Old Judge smoking tobacco, as well as Lorillard's Climax chewing tobacco.

Milt Joyce's Oriental Saloon was the scene of a shooting affray that took place on Sunday, at about 12:30 on the evening of October 10. It seems Johnny Tyler and John "Doc" Holliday had been in a shooting scrape earlier that evening but were separated and disarmed by mutual friends before anything serious happened. Joyce asked Tyler to leave the saloon, so he did. Holliday was also asked to leave, but refused. Joyce also "remonstrated" Holliday for creating a disturbance in the saloon. Deciding to leave, Holliday went to the bar and asked for his gun. He was refused his pistol, so he angrily left. Shortly thereafter, he returned with a "self-cocker." He spoke some words to Joyce and then fired his gun at him. Joyce, no more than ten feet away, jumped

Marshall Williams's store ad, 1880,
Tombstone Epitaph.

at Holliday and knocked him on the head with a six-shooter. However, before Joyce could stop him, Holliday managed to fire twice. The first shot hit Joyce in the hand, and the other struck Joyce's partner, Mr. Parker, in his big toe.[21] Joyce was taken out of the saloon, and Holliday was placed in a chair in the saloon. Because of Holliday's bloody appearance, those on hand thought his wounds severe, if not fatal. Seeing Holliday's wounds were not serious, Deputy Marshal Earp arrested him. He was charged with assault with a deadly weapon and intent to kill. Judge Reilly set his bail for two hundred dollars, which he promptly furnished. The bartender, Gus Williams, also known as James Augustus Rokohl, was arrested, too. In the confusion it was believed Gus had also fired a shot during the melee, but having no complaints against him, he was released. Shortly after his release, Williams was notified that his sister, Mrs. Thomas H. Selby, Jr., had passed away. He asked for the funeral to be postponed until he could arrive in San Francisco to attend. After this incident, William C. Parker, Jr., left Tombstone for good and returned to Oakland, California.

The Golden Eagle Brewery was in full swing by this time, and its owners, Wehrfritz and Tribolet, enjoyed success. The *Arizona Quarterly Illustrated* said, "As the quality of the beer manufactured by them gives admirable satisfaction to all their customers, and the demand for it exceeds their present capacity for supply, it is the intention of the owners to enlarge their premises. This is the pioneer brewery outside of Tucson."[22] Their homemade brew was sold for six dollars for ten gallons, three dollars for five gallons, three dollars for a dozen bottles, and one dollar for three bottles while in the saloon. Their brew was also delivered to patrons in a delivery wagon. Sigfried Tribolet, a native of Ertach, Berne, Switzerland, also held interests in the Red Jacket and Young America mines.

While beer was the specialty at the Golden Eagle, wine was featured at Miley's Sonoma Wine House at 519 Allen Street. They sold one bottle of Sonoma white or red wine for fifty cents; half bottles for twenty-five cents; per gallon eighty cents. California port, sherry, and Angelica wine, California grape brandy, Swiss, Limburger, and American cheeses were all available at Miley's. Holland herring, sardines, and cold lunches were also available. They advertised that they kept everything of the best kind at reasonable prices. They encouraged customers to call and see for themselves.

1881

A stroll down Tombstone's prosperous streets in early 1881 provided visitor and resident alike with a variety of saloons. On Allen Street, James Vogan renovated, improved, and renamed his saloon, formerly Vogan's Saloon. In mid-May, his new saloon, at the same location of 634 Allen Street, was called the Crystal Palace Saloon. Vogan announced the saloon's management had hired several young ladies to act as waitresses. He claimed, "No forward or immodest conduct will be allowed, and the saloon will be conducted strictly on general business principles, where good cheer will be dispensed to the convivial so long as they are courteous." He encouraged his former patrons to visit

LEASES.

MINING LOCATIONS

CRYSTAL PALACE
SALOON.

634 Allen Street, Tombstone.

JAMES VOGAN, - - - - Proprietor.

The old stand, known as "Vogan's Saloon," has
lately been

Renovated & Improved.

THE FINEST BRANDS OF

WINES, LIQUORS, CIGARS.

The Management has secured the services of
several young ladies to act as waiters. No forward
or immodest conduct will be allowed, and the
saloon will be conducted strictly on general business principles, where good cheer will be dispensed to the convivial so long as they are courteous.

Give the New Management a call and be convinced that it is a pleasure to be waited upon by
well-behaved young ladies.

Tombstone, May 20, 1881.

Crystal Palace
saloon ad, June
1881, Tombstone
Daily Nugget.

his new saloon to be convinced, and "to be waited upon by well-behaved young ladies."[23]

The Alhambra Saloon, now under new ownership, was quite direct in its advertising approach. "Checks, drafts, gold, adobes, and the larger the amounts the better, will be received daily that is, I would like to receive them."[24] Mellgren and Nichols also mentioned they ran the finest bar in the city and were open day and night.

The Schooner Saloon, at the corner of Seventh and Allen streets, took a different angle, using the Arizona heat as their ploy. Proprietors Fritz and Bill simply claimed the Schooner was the coolest place, had the coolest beer, the biggest glasses, and the finest lunches.

Another spot on Allen Street for refreshments was the Grand Hotel Bar. Jack Allman and W. W. "Tink" Tinker, formerly of Virginia City,

Old Port ad, from the author's collection.

Nevada, owned it. They advertised that mixed drinks were a specialty and ice cold drinks were made from the best imported liquors. On August 4, 1881, the *Daily Nugget* wrote, "Tink knows all the old 'Comstockers.'" Tinker later took charge of the Grand Hotel Bar in late April 1882.

Across the street from the Grand Hotel was the Cosmopolitan Hotel, which also provided its guests a saloon. Previously run by "Buckskin" Frank Leslie, the Cosmopolitan Saloon was now run by Robert H. Archer and R. J. Pryke. After taking over the saloon, the two refurbished it. Archer took the morning watch and mixed cocktails for his patrons, while Pryke handled the evening crowd. R. J. Pryke eventually left Tombstone for the Yukon country in Canada. Convinced there was nothing there worth taking, he returned to Tombstone in late November 1882. Archer remained in Tombstone and ran a saloon in town. By the end of the year, they were once again partners in a saloon at 409 Allen, near the old Cosmopolitan location.

While Fremont Street had its share of visible saloons, it also had one underground. Being closer to the mines than most, the Grotto was located beneath the county recorder's office on Fremont Street between Third and Fourth Streets. Otto Eschman and William B. Alderson, proprietors, offered fine beer, liquors, cigars, and imported lunches. Their imported lunches were said to have been "without compare," and were served by the "rapid" caterer, Hermann Dipow.[25] They also sold Fredericksburg beer, for which they were the sole distributors.

Tombstone's saloons acted as the stage for many colorful events. June 22, 1881, began innocently enough, but the Arcade Saloon, owned by Mr. Alexander and Mr. Thompson, was about to make Tombstone history. With warm weather, and a gentle, refreshing breeze, people moved about the day and tended to their normal duties until a loud clap of a thunderous nature interrupted them. It wasn't a storm though; it was an explosion.

Mr. Alexander, proprietor of the Arcade Saloon, located near the corner of Fifth and Allen Streets, had finally decided to have a barrel of condemned liquor shipped away. Before it could be shipped, however, he needed to measure the amount of liquor in the barrel. Using a gauge rod to measure the liquor, he accidentally dropped it into the barrel. His bartender, Mr. Hazelton, came out from behind the bar to retrieve the rod for him, carelessly bringing his lit cigar with him. Hazelton, for reasons unknown, also lit a match, and when the fumes from the liquor reached the open flame, there was an instantaneous explosion.[26]

Fortunately, no one in the saloon was injured, and everyone escaped through a back door. In less than three minutes the flames had reached the attached buildings, literally spreading like wild fire. People standing across the street from the saloon felt the blast, and some even sustained burns from the force of the explosion. The fire alarm was immediately sounded, but because of the lack of facilities for extinguishing the blaze, the fire grew out of control. People in adjoining businesses tried to retrieve their most important items from their buildings before they, too, were engulfed in the flames.

Tombstone was in a chaotic state. People tried to save their businesses by soaking them with water or covering them with wet blankets. Many tore down their front verandahs and awnings since these were prime targets for the spreading flames. Even the weather became Tombstone's enemy, as the thermometer reached one hundred degrees in the shade at four o'clock that afternoon. Before the fire subsided, it had burned everything east of Fifth Street to Seventh. It also crossed over to the north side of Fremont Street and to the south side of Allen Street to Toughnut Street before it was done.

By six o'clock, the area burned by the fire was no longer the thriving business area to which Tombstonians had grown accustomed. Instead, it was a charred, smoldering district where many lost their hopes and dreams. Some of the businesses lost were the Oriental Saloon, Arcade Saloon, Arcade Cigar Store, Lion Brewery, and Miley's Sonoma Wine House. Miley's Sonoma Wine House rose from the burnt debris in August, when it reopened at the old location, 523 Allen Street. Rafferty's Saloon was also lost, and shortly after the fire, John Rafferty and John Ahean announced the dissolution of the partnership. Rafferty did, however, place a notice saying he would resume the business at his old stand on 521 Allen Street as soon as the building was up. Also lost was the Key West cigar store, Fontana Dance House, Magnolia Saloon, Arizona Brewery, J. J. McClelland's store, Palace Saloon, Safford & Hudson Bank, the district court room, and many others. These businesses were only a handful of those lost. In all, about seventy-five were destroyed. While only a few business owners had insurance, many were able to rebuild what they had lost. Of the businesses mentioned, only one, the Fontana Dance House, had insurance. Their losses, estimated at three thousand dollars, were greater than the insurance on the building, which was only insured for one thousand dollars.

Once the charred remains stopped smoldering and the last flames flickered away, the debris was cleared. Some business owners had already telegraphed their suppliers for a new shipment of goods to be delivered immediately. Although the devastating fire claimed half of Tombstone's busy business district, the city had begun the rebuilding process almost as quickly as it had been destroyed.

New businesses and old businesses, many with new addresses, sprang up everywhere. On July 2, 1881, an announcement appeared in the *Daily Nugget* for the Capitol Saloon. Thomas Moses, formerly of Moses and Mehan's saloon, was its proprietor. Thomas's new saloon was located at the southwest corner of Fourth and Fremont.

Shortly after the fire, the grand opening of an old favorite was announced. Peter Spence and John Roberts announced they were opening Vogan's Saloon. They claimed they were a "two-bit house," which drew only the most select clientele. They also advertised that "square faro was dealt, and guests were treated with courtesy and respect."[27] The *Epitaph* said, "Ye hot and thirsty souls give them a call.

Tombstone tobacco ads, from the *Tombstone Epitaph*.

Vogan's opposite Wells, Fargo & Co." The new owners informed everyone they intended to make their saloon a place for all who appreciated first-class attention and "No. 1 liquid refreshment."

Although alcohol proved dangerous to Tombstone in the recent fire, it was later helpful for one man. Since it was a hot July afternoon, a worker at Carlisle S. Abbott's dairy ranch lay down to nap under a shed. After falling asleep, he was abruptly awakened, having been bitten by a tarantula. The spider bit him on the forefinger, which swelled horrifically. The swelling traveled to the man's hand and arm, and eventually his whole body was enlarged.[28] Mr. Abbott immediately cauterized the bite and soaked the man's body in ammonia and his diaphragm in whiskey. He was expected to make a full recovery.

Whiskey was just one of the items offered at the Bonanza Saloon, which was owned by I. Levi, who was new to Tombstone. Levi offered his patrons fine wines and liquors at wholesale and retail prices. He also announced there was a cigar store associated with the saloon. Levi bought the saloon from L. Enricht, who was forced to sell his saloon to Levi a few short months after he opened it. According to the

Arizona Daily Star, Enricht sold his saloon because of "financial embarrassments." It seems Mr. Enricht was carrying on with a nineteen-year-old woman he had brought to town with him, despite being married to another woman. Enricht first brought the young woman (her name was never revealed as a courtesy) to Tombstone a couple of months earlier. According to the *Arizona Daily Star*, "This unfortunate creature it is hereabouts currently stated that he seduced her in that city [San Francisco] under a promise of marriage, and with the assurance that he was an unmarried man, while all the time his wife and three children, who are here now, resided in that city."[29] A few short months later, Levi was running the Palace Saloon at 502 Allen Street. While he sold wine, liquor, and beer, Mr. Levi's specialty was still imported and domestic cigars. He also advertised he had an endless supply of "fancy goods" at bottom prices.

The Bank Exchange Saloon, now owned by Sultan and Arnold, was one of those announcing its grand reopening. The saloon was now in the old post office building at 220 Fourth Street, near the corner of Fremont. On July 14, the keno game at the Bank Exchange Saloon was moved to the Occidental Saloon, next door to Wells, Fargo & Co. Ike Isaacs was in charge of the games. Misters Cameron and Allender owned the Occidental Saloon, at 429 Allen, which was said to be crowded with "lovers of good whiskey."[30] Gus Williams tended bar. The saloon also contained a first-class restaurant called the Occidental Restaurant, which was run by Aristotle Petro.

The Arizona Brewery, located at 520 Allen Street, was waiting for its paint and plaster work to be done so it could begin filling its customers' glasses. On July 13, the brewery welcomed its customers back to a new and improved business. It contained "new appliances of the most improved kind."[31] Misters Bernhardt and Leptien announced they were once again selling San Francisco lager beer from the Philadelphia Brewery by the schooner.[32]

By mid-July Tombstone was on the rebuilding recovery road. A stroll through the streets of Tombstone found many old firms doing a substantial business in new, sturdier adobe structures. This was owing in part to a new city ordinance that prevented anyone within the city limits from building a wooden structure. Any new buildings in the city limits had to be constructed of brick or adobe.

The Grotto, being underground and west of Fourth Street, was untouched by the recent fire and continued serving Tombstone quality libations. One of its proprietors, William Alderson, retired from the business. While Alderson traveled to other mining communities, the Grotto remained a favorite place in town. It also served as a band practicing center. Tombstone's newly formed brass band consisted of mostly Englishmen. The band's leader was thirty-four-year-old Thomas Vincent. The first cornet was played by Frank Garland, the second by George Eddy, the third by H. Trevina, and the fourth by Charles Winslow. First alto was Richard Goldsworthy, and the second was Richard Fuzina. Frank Broad played the first trombone, Mr. Butler played the first E flat baritone, and William Vincent played the second E flat. Samuel Simmons completed the band with the bass drum.

The *Nugget*, being the tenant above the Grotto, printed this poem in its paper:

> Charlie 'Otto' Eschman, the boss of the snug little Grotto;
> Got to thinking it over, and thought that he ought to;
> Stroll up to the *Nugget*, and say with a smile;
> You're tired I know boys, just quit for a while;
> Pray let me invite you downstairs for a minute;
> I'm not jesting, on honor, you'll find something in it.
> Nothing loath, the whole office, including the devil;[33]
> In a trice were in front of his counter so level;
> And with schooners in hand of the landlord's best beer;
> Sung if it wasn't for Eschman we wouldn't be here;
> And like all of his patrons, adopted their motto;
> If you want a square drink, you must go to the Grotto.

Clara Brown noted Tombstone still sported its share of saloons and gambling halls when she wrote a story for the *Californian* in July 1881. She penned:

> Liquor and gambling saloons are a conspicuous feature of the streets, both in point of numbers, and elegance of finish. Strains of music issue from these attractive rooms, drawing in the idle crowd; and fortunate is he who goes no farther then to curiously scan the progress of the games. Some of those who participate therein, may leave with heavier pocket-books that were theirs when they went in, but the majority will depart with flat purses. It is an old saying that plenty of gambling is a sure indication of a prosperous camp. Professional gamblers will not

remain long where no profits are to be made, and that plenty of money is in circulation is a pretty good sign of abundant yielding mines. There were ten faro games in Tombstone, besides innumerable monte, keno, poker and snap games.[34]

The *Nugget* concurred with Clara's observations, and stated the city's recovery "is evidenced by the fact that the faro and keno games are nightly crowded." Faro, when dealt fairly, was called the "gentlemen's game." When the game was dealt "squarely," the percentage against the player and in favor of the bank was less than any other banking game. If it was not dealt fairly, a gambler had no more chance than "a cat in Hades without claws."[35] The *Nugget* claimed the faro games at Lou Rickabaugh's Oriental clubrooms were run like a funeral. A player walked up to the table, which was presided over by a gentlemanly dealer, and put down his bet, whether it was a quarter or a twenty-dollar piece. If he was lucky enough to win, he was paid fairly and without any retribution from the dealers. He was also asked to come back again.

Tombstone's legitimate saloons, which paid license fees, grew angry about the illegal Chinese gambling "dens" that popped up. There were numerous dens, and none of them were paying the monthly twenty-five-dollar gambling license fees. The *Nugget* called the situation to the attention of the public, asking whose duty it was to take care of such matters.[36] Most individuals who broke the law in Tombstone were forced to endure City Marshall Virgil Earp's newest idea. Many arrested for being drunk and disorderly, fighting, disturbing the peace, and other various crimes were forced to labor during their imprisonment. Earp formed a chain gang of prisoners and put them to work cleaning the city's streets.

Despite Earp's chain gang threat, people still broke the law. John Harker, proprietor of the Milwaukee Brewery, located between Seventh and Eighth Streets, was arrested in late July on an assault charge. A party named Burns filed a complaint against Harker for assaulting Burns's wife, Hannah. Mrs. Burns was said to be in a precarious state after the supposed beating. Harker said the charge was a malicious one and claimed Mrs. Burns had stumbled and fallen. He was released on a one-hundred-dollar bond, posted by Charley Tribolet, and was later acquitted of the charges. Burns was arrested for threatening Harker's life.

Despite Tombstone's hopeful future, pioneer saloon man Benjamin Cook left. He departed for his native Massachusetts earlier in the year to be married. Cook and his bride honeymooned in Salem. In early August 1881, he sent word back to Tombstone saying he would not be returning.

Unlike Cook, many people took advantage of Tombstone's cosmopolitan living conditions, as did the pesky fly. It continued to be bothersome, so the newspapers continued inserting jokes about their flying tenant. The *Nugget* devoted one half of their columns to a story of the fly. It was entitled, "The Fly," and began:

> It apparently has no reverence for age—as it has no endearing recollection of parentage. It will shut one eye, take good aim, and strike one on the end of the nose with the force of a battering ram. You drive it off, but before your arm has fallen to your side it strikes you again on the same spot, and repeats the operation until you are in a frenzy. It will then locate a tunnel site in your ear, and the rapidity with which it will bore through the porphyry dust will make you think there is a diamond drill at work driven by a 100-horsepower engine. It is also peculiarly in its tastes. It will insist on helping us read proofs, and we regret to say, occasionally places a period where only a comma was intended...We can only add, it is exceedingly the 'fly.'[37]

In another report the *Nugget* wrote, "A drunk stretched out on Fremont Street yesterday was covered with three million flies. There may have been a few more, but no less."[38]

Another annoyance in town, according to some, was a notorious accordion player. He was said to roam the streets and disturb many. The *Nugget* said, "The fiend who plays the self-destroying and murder provoking instrument in this neighborhood, will be cremated promptly, and his infernal machine turned over to the Chinese band."[39]

Regardless of minor aggravations, Tombstone was a town with pure water, a delightful climate, beautiful surroundings, and congenial people. With the richest mines in the country, mills springing up, new buildings going up like magic, and every evidence of a prosperous town, who would entertain ever leaving—at least that was the question posed by the *Nugget*.

One enterprising man, Mr. Hawkins, who chose to capitalize on Tombstone's glorious reputation, bought out Roderick Hafford's wholesale liquor business. His store was located on Fourth Street in the Tribolet block. Even though he sold his wholesale business, Colonel Hafford maintained his retail liquor business at his old stand in Brown's Hotel building. The genial Billy Knapp tended bar at Hafford's until the fire, then moved to John Maguire's Saloon and tended bar for him. By October 1881 though, Billy had moved to Benson and tended bar there.

Soda was another popular beverage in Tombstone, and it was used to make a variety of mixed drinks. Frederick Blush bought the Union Soda Works, at the corner of Second and Toughnut, from Valentine Mand on July 19 for nine hundred dollars. Included in the sale were the goods needed to run a soda manufacturing business and all the apparatus needed for making soda water, along with a horse and spring wagon. Mand had previously purchased Kelly's Wine House on Fremont Street. Almost one year after opening at his new location on Allen Street, Kelly had built a thirty-by-twenty-foot addition. The new home of Kelly's Wine House, located in Dillon & Kenealy's building, was to be completed by August 1, 1881.

Being in the liquor business had many risks; however, Mother Nature was not one usually associated with it. Many businesses felt the wrath of the summer monsoon season. The county recorder's office was one adobe building partially destroyed by the rains during that season. A wall adjoining this building was made of mixed adobes and could not stand the force of rushing water against it. The rain weakened the base, and the rest collapsed, falling into the basement. Otto Eschman, who operated the Grotto, a beer and German lunch hall, occupied the basement. Fortunately, no one was in the area where the wall fell and minimal damage was done. A horse shed at the O.K. Corral was also slightly damaged by the collapse. An awning over the Lion Brewery fell and crashed to the sidewalk, hitting William Morris, who was working on the building next door. His leg was badly bruised by the falling awning. Two pedestrians narrowly escaped the falling awning.

The Alhambra Saloon was the site of great excitement as the result of a big poker game. The admittance to the game was a double eagle, which was a twenty-dollar gold piece. It took five big river bits, or about one dollar and twelve and one-half cents, to see the first raise. Most of Tombstone's "pasteboard" veterans were on hand, including Dick Clark and Nick Stanton. A month later, a monte game caused some excitement at the Alhambra. About two o'clock in the morning on a September day, Fred Dodge, a well-known sport, got into a dispute over a monte game with a cowboy and fired his pistol at him or in the floor.[40] Just where Dodge aimed could not be determined, and before the smoke cleared, Officer Bronk entered the saloon. He did not, however, arrest either party.

Businesses like the Alhambra had more beverage choices when Hawkins, Boarman & Co. opened a large wholesale business on 116 Fourth Street. Their nearly full-page ad stated their newly opened store carried cigars and Louis Roederer and Haraszthy champagnes and that they were the sole agents for Blatz's Milwaukee beer. They also sold Milton Hardy's Old Reserve, Guinness Dublin stout, Ross, Belfast ginger ale, Sonoma claret, Ohio catawba, Cocumongo, and Angostura and Hostetter's bitters.

"Age is nothing, blood will tell," was the proverb used by the *Nugget* to describe Colonel Brown's Pony Saloon on Fourth Street. They claimed, "Everybody drinks there. Governor Stebbins, Con Cutler, and when the Colonel is in good nature, the impecunious *Nugget* reporter drinks there, too."[41]

In September, the Grand Hotel Saloon, presided over by Johnny Chenowith and Jack Allman, was renovated. When completed, the refurbished Grand was referred to as one of the handsomest and most tastefully fitted up saloons in the territory. The Grotto Saloon had originally opened in a basement under the *Nugget's* office. Destined to be a basement saloon, when the Grotto later collapsed from the rains, it relocated under the Grand Hotel. Some of the Grand's noted guests included Johnny Ringo, who stayed there on September 13, 1881, and Ike and Phin Clanton on September 22.

Another saloon's ad graced the papers on September 11 when the Elite announced its grand opening. Thomas F. Coghlan was the proprietor, and his establishment was located on the north side of Allen, between Fifth and Sixth Streets. He, like most others, offered choice liquors, beer, and cigars. Coghlan remained in the saloon business for a while, then tried his hand at Tombstone's favorite pastime—mining.

In November, Coghlan's saloon was the site where a longtime feud between Frank Dolan and Thomas Murphy ended with a gunshot. Facing each other in front of the saloon, the men exchanged words. Dolan drew his pistol and struck Murphy over the head. In doing so, Dolan's gun discharged, sending the bullet screeching into the night. As the two wrestled for possession of the gun, Officer Bronk arrived on the scene to separate them. Murphy ran into a nearby shoe store when the officer intervened. He was later apprehended and both men were arrested.

While it's true that playing with a pistol is dangerous, betting that it turned into a whiskey fountain was another matter altogether. It seems a local man tried this unfortunate idea in a Fourth Street saloon, and his gun accidentally discharged.

The Golden Eagle Brewery was one of Tombstone's first, and its owners, Ben Wehrfritz and Sigfried Tribolet, greeted many thirsty patrons during their reign. However, Ben and Sigfried decided to go separate ways in September 1881. Sigfried started his own saloon on Allen Street and took the Golden Eagle Brewery name with him. Ben stayed at their original location but renamed his saloon the Crystal Palace.

Tombstone's brass band continued to entertain residents, but now they had their own saloon in which to practice. Bandleader Thomas Vincent opened the Music Hall Saloon at 519 Allen Street. He advertised it was a cozy and peaceable place to get a cool drink. It was also touted as the headquarters for the Tombstone Band.

In addition to the Music Hall Saloon, there were about forty-five saloons, breweries, and liquor houses in Tombstone. The September 23, 1881, *Epitaph*, making light of this, said, "In the absence of an unlimited supply of saloons and places of amusement, the place next to the Grand Hotel, formerly occupied by Julius A. Kelly for a wine house, has been leased by other parties and is fitting it up as a shooting gallery and bowling alley. There will be a bar and cigar stand in front." In mid-October John D. Ahlers opened the Tivoli Saloon on 428 Allen Street. He also operated a restaurant at 203 Fourth Street.

No ordinary saloon, the Tivoli offered patrons a target gallery and bowling alley. Rules at the Tivoli were quite strict and were posted in the paper for all to see. Persons who were intoxicated, noisy, or turbulent were not allowed to appear in the target gallery to practice, nor were they allowed to bowl. If such individuals became obnoxious to the patrons or proprietor, they were asked to leave. Persons target shooting or rolling ten pins were given a ticket at the end of each game. They took this ticket to the bar and were supposed to pay before beginning another game. The cost of target shooting was twenty-five cents for six shots, and pool shooting was twenty-five cents for five shots. Patrons also participated in championship shooting for prizes daily, weekly, or monthly for twenty-five cents for four shots. The winner had the most bull's eyes during the day, week, or month. Bowling cost twelve and one-half cents for six boxes per man, and twenty-five cents for ten boxes per each man. Anyone complying with the rules of the Tivoli could bowl or shoot until eleven o'clock every night. Ahlers also offered five dollars and a free week's worth of bowling to anyone who made three hundred pins.

Smoking was very common in the late 1800s, so it's no surprise that the *Daily Nugget* printed a rather lengthy article about cigarettes. The article discussed how only a few years earlier, the majority of cigarettes smoked in America had been imported. In the last few years, however, more than 408 million American cigarettes were taxed. A writer from the *Philadelphia Times* reported there wasn't a cigarette made in America worth smoking. The *Nugget* reported that large fortunes were being made, while millions of people were slowly ruining their digestive organs by inhaling the "foul stuff." They challenged any smoker to visit a doctor and be examined after smoking a pack of cigarettes. Unfortunately, vitriol left no sinister impression on the tongue, throat, or palate. They also said, except for maybe one or two brands, every cigarette was a source of violent physical reaction. They claimed it was better to smoke a pound of tobacco in any other form than the pinch mingled with poison that makes up the ridiculously expensive and utterly worthless article of cigarette that holds the market. Regardless of what was being reported about tobacco, Mrs. L. C. Woodman opened a cigar store in October. Her advertisement appeared in the October 6 issue of the *Daily Nugget*. Her store was located in Barron's Barber Shop on Allen. She said she offered the finest brands of cigarettes, cigars, and tobacco in town, and at low prices.

Another woman to operate a business in town was Mrs. Maggie McKenna. Unfortunately, Mrs. McKenna failed to obtain a business license and was arrested for keeping a disorderly house without said license. She was sentenced to pay a fine of $92.75, including court costs. Ironically, an ad that ran underneath Maggie's arrest report read, "Attention Hooks!" A couple of weeks later, Maggie had more trouble in her saloon, which was "jest beyant the Epithet."[42] A couple of weeks later, Mrs. McKenna's name appeared in the paper again. The *Epitaph* began the article with, "Mother McKenna's bower was the scene of a little abnormal flurry...three shots were fired by some of the old lady's countrymen, but no damage was done, other than to scare the women and draw a large crowd of people."[43] Officer Flynn chased the shooter, but he disappeared into the shanties in Chinatown.

Colonel Hafford, of Hafford's Saloon, still conducted business in his usual manner. The *Nugget* claimed the place "maketh the heart of the dust-begrimed traveler glad on the arrival of the stage, and also the denizens of town, when they thirst after a pure quality of malt, extracts or common rye."[44] They also remarked the Colonel was always happy to see his friends and supply their wants with the best domestic and imported items available.

New businesses, including saloons, opened frequently in Tombstone. One belonged to Miss Mattie Webb, formerly known as Mattie Colby. Her Starlight Saloon, at 307 Allen Street, was formerly known as the Red Light. Mattie purchased the saloon in early 1881 from David Walters for twelve hundred dollars. She notified customers she had "regained" ownership of the saloon and requested old and new customers alike to patronize her saloon. She offered wines, liquors, cigars, and a nice quiet place to make a pleasant social call. Mattie's saloon should have been called a disorderly house, since women rarely operated anything else this low on Allen Street.

Despite recent publications on cigarettes, smoking remained quite popular during Tombstone's height, and many businesses vied for sales in town. Adolph Cohn & Bros., at 436 Allen, advertised it had all the popular brands of cigarettes, along with the best imported and domestic cigars in the market. It also offered smoker's articles, plug tobacco, and fancy goods in an endless variety to its customers. Cohn's cigar store was also the site of an odd event in mid-October. The *Nugget* wrote, "A fellow of infinite jest made a stump speech, delivered a sermon, scratched his back against a post, sat down in the street, and swallowed a raw egg. He did all this in fifteen minutes, and immediately after doing so, was labeled as insane."[45]

Since there were so many saloons in Tombstone, most proprietors tried to outdo the others by some means. Lou Rickabaugh & Co. once again opened an elegant saloon called the Oriental at the corner of Fifth and Allen Streets. They purchased a business license from the city, at a cost of thirty-five dollars, to operate two faro tables from July to October. Numerous patrons attended the grand opening and were entertained by Tombstone's brass band. The *Nugget* said, "The Tombstone brass band furnished some delightful music, echoed by the constant rattle of checks as the fearless sported with the 'tiger' in his luxurious abode."[46]

While Rickabaugh & Co. attracted patrons by offering a classy saloon, others tried different methods. Bob Hatch, of Campbell & Hatch's Saloon and Billiard Parlor, installed several old-fashioned, yet novel, barometers. The arrangement consisted of several frogs in large glass jars. When the weather indicated rain, they raised their voices. Bob went so far as to apply for a U.S. patent for his barometer. A few

weeks later, he had a fresh coat of white paint put on the walls, fres-
coed the ceiling, and repainted all the woodwork. They also appealed
to their customers by designing a billiard hall with the latest elegance.
They claimed they intended to pay strict attention to the comfort and
pleasure of their guests. John Caley was always on hand to minister to
their wants.

Sometimes barkeepers, like Caley, were jokingly referred to as
mixologists or pharmacists with a "medicine" chest. The *Epitaph*
wrote this little tidbit on the Grand Hotel Bar: "Should your appetite
go back on you today before you attempt to partake of the good
things about meal time, call in at the Grand Hotel Bar and consult Dr.
Jack Allman, and get him to mix you up something a little strengthen-
ing to tone up your stomach. Jack's medicine chest is full of the best
that money can buy, and he will fix your case sure."[47] The *Nugget* supposed the Grand Hotel Saloon was doing a good business, because
one of its owners, Jack Allman, sported a new diamond pin. The
Nugget said it was about the size of an egg, and, "When the light
strikes it you can't see anything of Jack, but inside of the room looks
as if the tail of a big comet was on exhibition."[48]

Not to be outdone by flashy Jack Allman and his diamond pin,
Colonel Roderick F. Hafford was said to have owned the largest and
finest Brazilian topaz on the Pacific Coast. It measured one inch long
by five-eighths of an inch broad and a quarter inch deep. It was set in
a ring of solid gold to correspond with the stone. Hafford's saloon business prospered, and so did Dan McCann and Fred Dodge's gambling
concession in the saloon. It was said they ran a quiet and square faro
game there.

Keeping up with their competition, the Leigh brothers, owners of
the Headquarters Saloon at 323 Allen Street, renovated their business.
"A way up time," is how the *Nugget* described the reopening on
November 4, 1881. They now offered patrons a reading room, with files
of all the latest periodicals. To entice patrons to join them, they offered
a free lunch, including roast pig. A few weeks later, the local paper
said the Headquarters Saloon was a local favorite.[49]

Not to be bested, Ben Wehrfritz, of the Crystal Palace Saloon,
remodeled his saloon and provided his customers with some very fine
music during the evenings. Thomas Corrigan, longtime saloon owner,
opened a new establishment at 504 Allen Street. The *Nugget* said, "Of
course, Tom's many friends will make it a point to call and sample his
stock and see that none of his beverages are allowed to spoil for lack

of patronage."[50] Corrigan, known for his extensive drink stock, also offered his own special drink. He was the sole patentee for a drink called Huachuca Punch.

Even though Corrigan's business was thriving, his personal life was struck by tragedy. On Sunday, November 13, 1881, Tom's wife attempted to take her own life for the third time. In an interview with her after the attempt, Mrs. Corrigan said she had been despondent and discouraged, so she took a nickel-plated, .41-caliber, self-acting Colt revolver, placed it to her head, and pulled the trigger. Several people heard the gunshot and rushed to the room, where they found her unconscious. Dr. Matthews was sent for and, upon his arrival, found the bullet had entered the right side of the head. It went in just above the ear, passed beneath the skin toward the front of her face, and hit the bone above her right eye. The bullet came out through her forehead, and was later found embedded in a wall in the room. While the injuries to Mrs. Corrigan were not fatal, Dr. Matthews was forced to remove her right eye the following day. The following month, on December 22, 1881, Thomas Corrigan left Tombstone for Mexico. He was employed as foreman by the Santa Maria Mining Company in Sonora, Mexico, where he joined up with his brother William and Thomas Shanahan. After working the mines for seven months, the trio, with their burros and supplies, moved on. Braving the avenging Apaches, the three men reached the Sierra Madre, about forty-five miles east of Sahuaripa, at Teopre, an old Mexican settlement. This area was historically known for its productive gold mine and richness of its placers, so Corrigan and his party remained, in search of gold and silver.

Back in Tombstone, pianos were becoming popular in many of Tombstone's saloons. Both the Oriental Saloon and the American Eagle Brewery sported one. The Oriental became the center of attraction when it not only offered piano music, but hired one of the best lady pianists on the coast. Miss Emma Howe, from San Francisco, entertained many patrons at the Oriental. The *Nugget* said, "And when a man loses his last chip his troubled soul may be calmed by the soothing strains of sweet music, or for that matter, by the sweeter smiles of the fair performer who dishes out the music by handfuls at the Oriental."[51]

Other sounds rose from the Oriental Saloon on the afternoon of November 15. A "difficulty" arose between owner Lou Rickabaugh and a man named C. D. Dill. The *Nugget* said, "The choicest of Arizona adjectives arose dove-like on the air, filling it with a blue and sulfuric haze, which would have filled the profanest type of bull-whacking tribe with calm complacency."[52] This affray was caused by a business difficulty between the two men. It was abruptly terminated when Dill drew his pistol and struck Rickabaugh on the head. The force of the blow caused the gun to fire, but the wayward bullet did not injure anyone. It first struck the awning post on Adolph Cohn's cigar store, passed into another porch six inches away, and then headed for the Grand Hotel's porch. It eventually hit a post in Kelly's Wine House and fell to the ground. Officer Flynn arrested C. D. Dill for carrying deadly weapons. He appeared in court, pled guilty, and paid a twenty-dollar fine plus court costs, for a total of twenty-five dollars. He was also charged with assault with a deadly weapon and attempted murder.

The Grand Hotel bar's proprietor, "Flashy" Jack Allman, was once again teased about his trendiness. Jack, who had been known to wear new fashions and sport elegant diamond jewelry, now sported a pearl, instead of his diamond. A millionaire friend in Paris wrote to Jack and told him diamonds were out of fashion and pearls were all the rage. Jack, fashionable man that he was, purchased a magnificent black cat's-eye pearl. He removed his diamond tiepin and replaced it with his new pearl. After a few days of wearing his trendy pearl, he was heard saying it would cost him too much for coal oil to light the Grand Hotel Bar, and it looked so dismal, many persons thought the place was closed for repairs. Fashionable or not, Jack went back to sporting his diamond headlight. In late November, Jack Allman and his partner, Johnny Chenowith, dissolved their partnership. Chenowith was responsible for collecting and paying all bills associated with their business and became sole proprietor of the Grand Hotel Bar.

Across the street from the Grand was Albert Fortlouis's Cosmopolitan Cigar Store at 411 Allen Street. Fortlouis had just arrived home from San Francisco, where he procured the finest selection of cigars (including the famous Key West), Meerschaum goods, and cigarettes ever brought to the territory—at least according to Fortlouis. He offered Henry Clay, La Modesta, Villaio, Grenadeni, Anthony and Cleopatra, and many other high-grade cigars. On November 28, 1881, German native Albert was granted U. S. citizenship. Albert also served in the U. S. Army for ten years, then received an honorable discharge.

Drinking stories frequently appeared in Tombstone's papers, and the *Nugget* printed one about a Wisconsin man. While standing at the top of a staircase, he advised a friend not to drink. As he turned, he fell down the stairs and broke his leg. The paper said, "This is a warning to you never to advise anyone not to drink." The paper also ran another "drinking" story in the same column. "'What do you mean coming home like this at 3 o'clock in the morning, drunk on hot whiskey punches, while I have nothing home but cold Sycamore water?' This is the manner in which she addressed him, as he leaned up against the bed post and vainly attempted to wind his watch with the bootjack, he answered: 'Hic—why don't you (hic), don't you warm it?' And there is a fine prospect for a divorce."[53]

1882

Mr. Joyce, once again the owner of the Oriental, had a grand levee at his saloon in early January 1882 to celebrate his reacquisition of the saloon. Lou Rickabaugh & Co. had sold the Oriental to Joyce, who previously owned it with William Parker, before the Doc Holliday incident. Joyce advertised, "Once more to the front. Having again become proprietor of this old and popular establishment will continue, as in the past, to furnish the best brands of wines, liquors and cordials to be had in the market." In addition to "all kinds of games being conducted in an honest and gentlemanly manner," he offered vocal and instrumental music every night.[54] The *Epitaph* said, "It is nightly thronged by men seeking recreation after their day's labor is over. It is again becoming the headquarters of mining men and visitors from abroad, who are sure to meet with those whom they most desire to see. The music, instrumental and vocal, adds largely to the attractions of the place. Outside of San Francisco there is not a nicer place in the country than the Oriental."[55] Just as Joyce was taking over the Oriental, Ben Maynard and Lou Rickabaugh were arrested for disturbing the peace. A couple of days later, Rickabaugh pled not guilty and the charges were dismissed, but Maynard was fined ten dollars.

Even though Tombstone and its saloons obtained ice from a factory in nearby Charleston, it was still expensive. In January 1882, Mr. William K. Leveridge, former superintendent of the Tombstone Water, Mill & Lumber Company, offered an alternative. It was Mr. Leveridge who had brought cheap water to Tombstone, and he was doing the same with ice. His idea was backed by several wealthy San Francisco businessmen and supported by the heaviest consumers in Tombstone. Consumers of ice paid five cents per pound, but would soon pay just three and one-half to four cents per pound. When the Tombstone Ice Works made this announcement, the Tombstone &

Charleston Ice Company said it was adding new machines and intended to charge three cents per pound in the near future. Forty-five Tombstone consumers signed one-year contracts with Leveridge. He also sold ice to families for the same price, saying ice was a necessity in every household.

A three-ton, low-pressure binary absorption machine was already ordered from H. Bloomfield, who was the San Francisco agent for the New York Ice Machine Company. This ice company owned the French patents for the ice machines. The substance used to freeze the ice was a compound of ethyl-sulphurous-dioxide. It froze eight-inch thick solid blocks in twenty-four hours. The ice works were built in Watervale, but the company had an office in Tombstone, and by May 1, 1882, Tombstone had affordable ice. A new ice plant, with cheaper prices, meant businesses and families alike could prevent meat, fruits, and other perishable commodities from spoiling.

On the heels of an ice factory being talked about in town, the Bureau Saloon, formerly known as the Red Rock Saloon, opened on Allen Street between Fifth and Sixth Streets on January 19, 1882. Owners Michael Gaffney and L. Robinson said, "We notify the public that we have taken a new departure. Believing that success depends upon small profits and large businesses, we have secured advantages of purchases of the best liquors, wines and cigars to be found in Tombstone, from first-class, cash wholesale houses abroad, at rates impossible to be procured by any other saloon in Tombstone. Nothing but the best of everything on hand. Wines and liquors for medicinal purposes a specialty. Call and test for yourselves. Comfortable rooms! Polite attention! Best Stock!"[56]

Even though smoking was generally accepted, and sometimes expected, some city council members did not agree. In early February, while council was in session, member Flynn and clerk Chapin began smoking. The mayor immediately ordered them to quit. A motion was then made to suspend the rules so smoking could be allowed, but the motion was defeated. The mania to indulge overcame the gentlemen, and they began smoking again. Mr. Thomas again moved that the council be allowed to smoke during sessions. Mr. Dean seconded the motion, and a vote was taken; however, the result was the same. The vote was reconsidered and members Thomas and Dean voted aye, Thomas Atchison voted no, and Mr. Nash remained silent. The mayor voted no to the smoking motion, so quiet Alderman Nash was forced to vote and said aye. Mr. Thomas asked that the motion not be put on the books, but Atchison strongly objected and argued, "that we make a smoking room of the city hall" be properly noted in the minutes. It was so ordered.[57]

It was well-known that the heart of Tombstone's business district was found on Allen Street, between and Third and Sixth Streets, but there was also a large number of businesses situated on Fremont Street. The business district was supposed to have been on Fremont, but the most successful and popular businesses found their way to Allen. A business could really be set up anywhere, except for certain ones that were not allowed in the business district. The city council passed an ordinance stating anyone could legally operate a house or room of ill-fame or prostitution, so long as they paid the proper license fees and were in the proper location. The proper location, specifically spelled out, wove around the popular business district. It began at the southern part of Tombstone, on Eighth Street, and traveled there, 150 feet north of Allen. It then paralleled Allen to Sixth, back down to Allen halfway and traveled along Allen to Fifth Street until it reached Toughnut. It then went west on Toughnut until it reached Third, then traveled north, fifty feet above Allen, then west paralleling Allen to First Street. Basically, anything east of Eighth Street and west of Second was acceptable. However, parts of Sixth and Seventh Streets on Allen were restricted. They got closer to the business district when they were allowed on Allen Street between Third and Fifth.

The restriction ordinance didn't last very long, and houses of ill-fame or prostitution were allowed anywhere in Tombstone. Outraged by the lack of ordinance enforcement, a woman sent a letter to the editor of the *Epitaph*. She wrote:

It seems from your issue of the 9th that the city fathers have extended in the demi monde the liberties of the city. Allen Street was virtually theirs, to such an extent that a respectable woman would hesitate to even cross it. But this was not enough. Hitherto, although it has been impossible to pass along the streets provided with sidewalks without our ears being stunned with a multitude of oaths 'at every turn' we have at least been allowed certain limits for a retired house, where little children could run and play without danger of such contamination. Tombstone is generally a fenceless city, and while it is difficult to restrain live children in a little lot, treeless, fenceless, and unattractive, we have felt secure at least in a respectable neighborhood. This, it seems, is now to be denied us, and owners of real estate are to be defenseless against the incursions of the vilest element of the community. Is it possible there are not righteous men left to save the city? Where are all the churches and their pastors? Are they, too, joined to the cowboy element, or are they with closed eyes and ears descending upon the wickedness of King Ahab and lamenting the fall of Sodom and Gomorrah? May we not at least petition this august body to define certain limits to restrict the respectable people, if they are so sadly in the minority?

It was signed, "A Mother."[58]

Almost as if to prove a point, a soiled dove of the *barrio libre* raised a ruckus on Allen Street near Fifth in early March.[59] She was escorted by two strong police officers to jail so she could have a place for calm meditation until she sobered up. The following day, the mayor and common council charged Bertha Martin with soliciting prostitution.

The Oriental Saloon was given a boost in late March when the *Epitaph* wrote a brief note about it. The reporter claimed the view from the Oriental was the finest to be had in Tombstone or any other city. From the southwest corner of the Oriental's porch, looking diagonally down Fifth, was a picturesque scene. In the forefront were the rolling hills lying between Tombstone and Charleston, and beyond the San Pedro river were the snow-capped peaks of the Huachuca mountains. Above all of this beauty was the blue "Italian" sky for which Arizona was noted. The *Epitaph* wrote, "The Oriental is a daisy."[60]

Former Tombstone resident William B. Alderson arrived to learn Tombstone's population had grown to about six thousand. Once proprietor of the Grotto Saloon on Fremont Street, he returned to his first love, according to the *Epitaph*. After months of traveling through Utah, Idaho, and Montana, he came back to Tombstone saying, "No mining district in the North compares to Tombstone."[61] Ironically, Alderson and Mr. Grattan opened a saloon under the Grand Hotel, which was also at one time called the Grotto. They renamed the saloon the Fountain and served an elegant lunch at their grand opening. A three-piece orchestra also entertained their new patrons. The Grand Hotel had another new bar open, but it was upstairs in the hotel. The bar in the Grand Hotel opened on March 20, 1882, and was managed by thirty-three-year-old Julian Piercy.

Imported beer was much anticipated in Tombstone, so when a saloon received a shipment, it made news. Ben Wehrfritz of the Crystal

Palace Saloon made his own brew, but he also imported beer from a variety of places. He received a train carload of Fredericksburg lager from San Jose, California, and had it on tap for his customers. He advertised, "Bock beer at the Fredericksburg Beer Depot. Grand Free Lunch! King Gambrinus' Day! Bock Beer for 2 Weeks."[62] Ben not only sold a variety of beers, but also made his saloon a showpiece. The paper described the Crystal Palace as having a "whole menagerie" on display, including an aquarium with beautiful goldfish. Wehrfritz's saloon also sported a new porch on the Fifth Street side.

Another bar, the Tivoli, announced it was the only place in Tombstone where one could get the celebrated Boca beer. Boca beer, noted for its quintessence of barley corn and hops, was made with Sierra snow. The *Epitaph* said, "Boca cheers but does not inebriate."[63] John D. Ahlers, manager of the Tivoli, placed the same size ad as competitor Ben Wehrfritz did. Directly under Ben's ad, Ahlers claimed, "A Beer Excitement in Tombstone. Everyone claiming the bonanza. After trying all the so-called lager beer in other places, call at the Tivoli for a glass of Boca, which is made of the Truckee River water, the best water on Earth, and is the only genuine draught in Tombstone. A FREE LUNCH to all who spend money at the bar."[64]

Wholesale liquor merchant, John McLelland, also offered Tombstone beer drinkers a real novelty. He received a full carload of New Jersey Feigenspan & Co.'s lager at his 506 Allen Street store. This shipment, which he had ordered four months before, was a rare treat for Tombstone. Even in New Jersey, where it was brewed, it was difficult to obtain. Many of the top judges rated this beer A number one. Its most notable qualities were mildness and clearness, and its taste had no equal.

It was a dusty, windy day when Julius A. Kelly sold all the furniture from his residence on April 27 to the highest bidder. On the same day, Mr. and Mrs. Kelly sold their house, near the corner of Ninth and Fremont Streets, to Ben Goodrich for five hundred dollars. C. C. Lipps, of Los Angeles, purchased Mr. Kelly's entire business stock and carried on Kelly's saloon business.

In early May, only seven saloons or bars made the "business directory" section of the *Epitaph*. There were many other saloons, bars, and cigar shops in Tombstone, but the *Epitaph* only listed the ones that advertised in their paper: Hawkins, Boarman & Co. on Fourth, between Allen and Toughnut streets; the Leigh brothers' Headquarters Saloon; Milton Joyce's Oriental; the Dragoon Saloon, operated by Patrick W. Lynch; the Dividend Saloon on Allen, formerly known as the Fashion Saloon, of which David Lynch and John O'Neil were also the proprietors; the Capitol Saloon at the corner of Fourth and Fremont with Thomas Moses still in charge; and Campbell and Hatch were still operating a billiard parlor and saloon. Most saloons sold cigars, but there were cigar and tobacco stores as well. B. J. McGinniss had his cigar stand in the Oriental Saloon, and A. Cohn & Bros. were still at their store on Allen street.

Milton Joyce of the Oriental Saloon was in the midst of performing a charitable act for a needy family. Joyce had *The Awakening*, an expensive oil painting, hanging over his bar. Depicting a nude woman awakening from sleep, it was described as very realistic and worth over one hundred dollars. Joyce volunteered to raffle this painting off in a drawing. He sold one-dollar tickets and the proceeds went to a local woman named Mrs. Wyxtrum, whose husband had been killed in a well in April. Incidentally, John Wyxtrum was buried twice—once in Boothill and then again when he was moved to the new City Cemetery in 1883.

Competing with imported beer, Sigfried Tribolet's brewery advertisements tempted the thirsty soul with his own Golden Eagle Brewery beer. The top of his advertisement read, "Patronize Home Industry." He also claimed the brewery, "Is now prepared to furnish families and saloons with the best beer brewed on the coast. Having established a reputation second to none, our patrons can rest assured that our beer will be of the best quality and at prices to suit the times. Schooner— twelve and one-half cents, bottle—twenty-five cents, or three bottles for fifty cents."[65, 66]

As Tombstone basked in the glow of a recent mining review, another devastating fire swept through the town. On May 25, 1882, a fire broke out in a rear water closet in the Tivoli Saloon. Its flames immediately touched the wooden walls and traveled to the saloon's framework. The ravenous fire hungrily consumed numerous shanties surrounding the saloon. Next came the apartments of the luxurious Tombstone Club, then the beautiful Grand Hotel and its saloon. In less than fifteen minutes, every business between Fourth and Fifth and Allen and Toughnut was charred ruins. The firemen tried to control the flames, but without the strength of good water pressure, the flames were too strong. Fortunately for Tombstone, the wind was not blowing with its usual gale force. Firemen and business owners began tearing down awnings and porches and doused their buildings with buckets of water.

The fire crossed Allen Street and devoured the Occidental, Hafford's, and Alhambra saloons. It then reached the Cosmopolitan Hotel, Brown's Hotel, and the Crystal Palace Saloon. Traveling down

Fourth Street, the fire reached the gun shop, and several explosions were punctuated by the screams of men, women, and children. It then crossed Fourth Street and Levinthall's clothing store on the corner of Fourth and Allen was destroyed. The flames traveled north to Fremont and devastated the *Nugget*'s office, as well as all other buildings in that vicinity. Once it reached Fremont, though, the fire was dynamited to stop its progress. After the last flame flickered out, Tombstone's losses exceeded five hundred thousand dollars.

The *Epitaph* wrote a poignant editorial a couple of days after the fire:

> Such has been the effects of the most destructive conflagra-
> tion that has yet visited Tombstone. Its depressing effect on
> the camp cannot be denied, but we feel sure that the
> depression will only be temporary and that the burnt district
> will be rebuilt and in a more solid and substantial manner
> than ever before. Already preparations are being made for
> the erection of fireproof structures. So long as the marvelous
> mines of this camp continue to send forth their treasure, so
> long will the town of Tombstone exist and flourish. Although
> it may experience many a setback, the wealth that lies hid-
> den in the treasure vaults which surround it will give life,
> vim, and vigor to its people. Their buoyant spirit and uncon-
> querable energies will rise above the accidents of fortune,
> and their manhood and untiring energy are bound to com-
> mand success...The resources which have built up the most
> flourishing camp in the territory are still here, and will yet
> make this town of Tombstone the Virginia City of the
> Southwest. Let us not repine about the past which cannot be
> recalled; but let us resolutely turn our faces to the future
> which makes all things even.[67]

Fortunately, most of Tombstone's business owners had insurance. The Grand Hotel and its tenants suffered losses amounting to $15,000, but had $6,000 of insurance coverage. Ben Wehrfritz of the Crystal Palace Saloon, who was completely wiped out, lost $23,000 and only had $8,000 in insurance. George Spangenberg, of Spangenberg's Gun Shop, suffered a loss of $6,000, but was well insured for $5,950. C. C. Lips, who had just taken over Kelly's Wine House, and Campbell and Hatch were each insured for $3,000 and suffered damages of $4,000.

John Ahlers's Tivoli Saloon, where the fire began, suffered losses of $5,000, and had coverage of $1,700. Grotto saloon owners Alderson and Grattan suffered $1,000 worth of damages, and had no insurance. Adolph Cohn's cigar stand lost $8,000, but had insurance to cover half the damages. Adolph stayed in Tombstone until late 1886 when he moved to Los Angeles and opened a store. While the Oriental Saloon was not destroyed, it suffered $2,000 in water and other damages, but Joyce was fully insured.

David Lynch and John O'Neil's Dividend Saloon, which was burned in the fire, moved into Julius Kelly's old place a month later, in June. They capitalized on Kelly's old reputation and placed an ad apprising readers they were at Kelly's old stand. They claimed that Kelly's old place had been refitted and had two elegant billiard tables. Colonel Roderick "Old Time Rox" Hafford went back into the saloon business about six months after the fire when he rented the premises of 417 Allen Street, next door to Campbell & Hatch's Saloon and Billiard Parlor.

To ensure customers could find their businesses, store owners filled the papers with notices advising patrons of their new locations. The Sultana cigar store announced it had relocated to 506 Allen Street in Eippert's barber shop. The Occidental Restaurant, with a new chef, relocated from Allen Street to Fifth Street. The paper was also filled with "Lost" ads for items either stolen or misplaced during the recent disaster.

Saloon owners began restocking their businesses and ordered their liquor from a variety of places, which often included agents in California. One such company was Moore, Hunt & Co. in San Francisco. When ordering their libations, saloon owners chose from AA, A, B, or C brands. They also received discounts when they ordered in large quantities, such as cases or barrels. Moore, Hunt & Co. not only specialized in Kentucky whiskey, but they also sold Anchor champagne and Crown whiskey. A barrel or half barrel of AA brand whiskey cost four dollars per gallon, while the same amount of C brand cost only three dollars.

In mid-June, a little scrap occurred at the Oriental Saloon, which was in full swing again after the fire. About ten o'clock in the evening, a ruffian named John Archer walked into the Oriental and grossly insulted Mr. Dean, the piano player. Dean ordered the man out of the saloon, but he refused, so Dean used force to make him comply. Archer struggled violently and fell just as he got to the front door. The policemen came upon the scene at that moment and arrested both men. While the officers were occupied, Archer again attacked Dean, striking him heavily over the eye. The officers finally got Archer under control and sent him to the cooler.

A little over a month after the 1882 fire, town merchants busily put finishing touches on their new buildings. It was the eve of the grand opening of Ben Wehrfritz's Crystal Palace, and his "new" saloon was a showpiece. The new structure was 80 by 120 feet and cost eighty-five hundred dollars. Wehrfritz used the front of his building as a beer hall and gambling saloon, which contained a water fountain in its center where goldfish swam. Frank Beluda used the back half of the building, fronting Fifth, as a barbershop. Next to that was the Rockaway Oyster House.

Adjoining the Crystal Palace on Allen Street was the Alhambra. Saloon owners Thomas Nichols and Joseph Mellgren reopened in early July, complete with new paint and furniture. Their saloon was also adorned with two splendid oil paintings of thoroughbred horses. By the end of the year, Mellgren had left the business, and longtime gambler Dick Clark purchased it. Nichols tended bar, while gaming expert Clark presided over the betting activities. Down Allen Street was Campbell & Hatch's Saloon and Billiard Parlor. Mr. Campbell recently returned from San Francisco where he purchased new billiard tables and a complete stock of fixtures. While Campbell was away procuring items for the business, Hatch remained at the saloon.

Across Allen on the former site of the Grand Hotel was Comstock & Brown's new one-story building, which cost them ten thousand dollars. The men chose not to rebuild the Grand Hotel, since Brown's Hotel and the Cosmopolitan Hotel were supposed to be rebuilt. Feeling another hotel was not needed; they leased part of the building to Leslie F. Blackburn and William Burdett, who opened the Senate Saloon. Blackburn, in addition to being a marshal in town, held the title of foreman in the Tombstone Fire Department. By the end of the year Blackburn had taken on a new partner, Charles Edelman, in his saloon. When they first applied for their business license, it had Blackburn's name on it, but he was then crossed off and replaced with Edelman & Co. The Senate Saloon's barroom at 426 Allen was forty-two feet deep and had four cardrooms in the back. The other part of the building was leased to Isaac "Little Jakey" Jacobs, who opened a restaurant. The old Grand Hotel's basement continued to play host to William Alderson and Grattan's Fountain Saloon and lunchroom. They applied for a business license from July to September 1882 at a cost of $6.70. The Fountain Saloon claimed it served the finest imported San Francisco lunches, including *pate de fois gras*, and advertised imported beer on draught or in bottles.

In June, the Grand Hotel's building owners, Fielding Brown and Sylvester Comstock, borrowed some money—$5,000 from Milton Clapp and Anson P. K. Safford and $3,970.11 from L. W. Blinn Lumber Company. The money was used to complete the rebuilding of the hotel. Brown and Comstock had until March 7, 1883, to repay the debts with interest. If they failed to repay the loans, the building would be sold, and the money divided among the lenders. When the loans were paid in full, the property would be reconveyed to them. Three months later, Comstock's family arrived and called Tombstone home. A year later, Comstock and his family were residing in Toyah, Texas. It is unknown whether the debt was repaid. The hotel was never built.

On June 22, 1882, the city council passed ordinance number forty-three, which was an amendment to section twenty-six of ordinance number four. Ordinance number four governed the licensing of businesses in the city of Tombstone and was originally approved April 5, 1881. This ordinance specifically said, "For each and every person who shall deal, play, carry on or open, or cause to be dealt, carried on or opened, or who shall conduct either as owner or employee, whether for hire or not any game of faro, Monte, roulette, lansquenet, rouge et noir, rondeau, keno, twenty-one, or draws or lottery, or any other kind of banking game of whatever name, played with cards, dice or any other device, whatever the game be played for money, checks, credit or any other valuable thing or representative of value, the monthly license is twelve dollars and fifty cents."[68]

In late June 1882, James J. Lane, former manager of the Eureka Restaurant, and Charles Blair, owner of the Way-Up Lodging House, opened the Way-Up Saloon. It was located near Sixth in the building where Mrs. Alexander's dressmaking store had stood before the fire. About eleven o'clock one early July morning, people on Allen Street were startled by gunfire from the Way-Up Saloon. One of the saloon's owners, James Lane, was the target. Earlier that day, Lane had been warned a certain female was carrying a pistol with his name on it. At ten o'clock that morning, Lane met the fiery woman on Fifth Street, near Allen. They spoke, and a nonviolent resolution was found. This, however, was not to Joe Price's liking; he had purchased the pistol for the anonymous female to shoot Lane and was not happy with her handling of the situation. He claimed to have overheard Lane malign the woman's character.

Price went after Lane, who had proceeded to work at his Way-Up Saloon after meeting with the offended woman. Price stood in the saloon's doorway and called Lane out. Price was informed Lane would not speak with him and did not want anything to do with him. Price then became offensive and called Lane a "damned old liar."[69] Lane did not like being called a liar, and he ran behind the bar, presumably to arm himself. However, before Lane could reach his gun, Price began shooting at him. Price missed his target but managed to knock down a stack of bar glasses.

Price fired four more shots, but Lane took cover behind a sturdy card table. After the last shot was fired, Lane jumped fifteen feet and landed in a back room. Price, out of bullets, ran down the street but was quickly apprehended by Officer Solon. Lane was arrested too, but was immediately released once details of the incident were revealed. Price was brought before Judge Wallace the following day, but Lane refused to press charges. Price was released after he paid the court costs.

Two months later, Lane again found himself in an altercation at the Way-Up Saloon. This time, Jerry McCormack was the source of Lane's troubles, which included a broken arm. Early in the evening, McCormack and Lane had become verbally abusive to one another. About four or five in the morning, McCormack left and headed for the Cornish Saloon. Lane followed him with the intention of whipping him, but Jerry took his stick and pummeled Lane severely, breaking his arm at the elbow. Both men were arrested, but Lane was subsequently released, and it was feared he would be crippled. McCormack, who was a slave to morphine, was experiencing serious withdrawal and had to be moved to the hospital where, coincidentally, Lane was resting.

Even though saloons and gaming halls competed for business, the saloon's extras were what attracted prospective visitors. To tempt guests, saloon owners offered a variety of entertainment and an endless selection of spirits. Pool and billiard tables were an integral part of both saloons and pool halls. California companies often placed ads in Tombstone's newspapers advertising a variety of goods, including pool tables. The J. M. Brunswick and Balke Company, of San Francisco, placed a large notice in the *Epitaph* saying they were the most extensive billiard and pool manufacturers in the world. Not to be outdone,

P. Liesenfeld, also of San Francisco, placed a similar ad. The company claimed it was the sole agent for the only genuine patented steel plate cushion, which was guaranteed for ten years. Liesenfeld moved to a smaller office, enabling him to claim he sold his tables cheaper than any other house on the Pacific coast.

Other businesses from San Francisco advertised for Tombstone's business, including liquor dealers, cigar stands, jewelry stores, and piano companies. The Read & Thompson Piano Company of St. Louis claimed to be notable for its remarkably sweet-toned pianos. Superior in workmanship, and made of genuine rosewood cases, the pianos were beautifully finished. Mr. A. Redewill, an agent for many of the leading piano companies in the country, sold Knabe, Pease & Irving, and Decker pianos. All came with warranties, a popular benefit, as the pianos suffered great heat and dust stress in Tombstone. Mr. Redewill annually polished and tuned each piano sold. Redewill must not have been the only agent, or he would have been very busy.

Many a cigar was smoked during Tombstone's boom, so it was good news when George Walker's Key West cigar store advertised it could be found on Allen, between Fifth and Sixth Streets in late July. Walker stated he received a large invoice of the celebrated Stratton & Storm's Bouquet cigars, Key West brand, and the Grand Central cigar. He also carried a full line of smoker's supplies, including meerschaum and brierwood pipes. Next door to the cigar store stood the Key West Saloon, owned by James Brophy. Brophy sold wine, liquor, and cigars to wholesale and retail markets. He also offered A. L. Blatz beer.

Albert Fortlouis maintained his Cosmopolitan Cigar Store where the hotel once stood, with clerk Jake Sichel at the counter. As Sichel went about his daily duties, a cranky, unknown customer came into the store around noontime on a hot August day. This "John Doe" became unruly, so Sichel escorted him from the store. As soon as they reached the sidewalk, John Doe jumped on Sichel and began to beat him, but he was no match for Sichel. Sichel immediately took control of the fight and had beaten his attacker several times before Officer Coyle arrived on the scene. Both men were arrested, and John Doe was fined ten dollars, while Sichel was acquitted.

The Delta Saloon was the happening spot one Sunday afternoon in late July 1882. New to the silver city, James Wilson wandered into the Delta for a drink. While enjoying his favorite libation, he noticed James Thompkins showing off his pistols to some "Mexicans" in the saloon. Since he was new, Wilson took the opportunity to show off in front of the spectators in the saloon. Just a little over twenty years old, he took one of the guns from Thompkins and began to "flourish" it. As he began to show the "Colorado cowboy plan of practicing for sheriff," which included swinging the pistol around the forefingers with rapidity and setting at the ready each revolution, the gun went off.[70] Despite warnings to be careful, Wilson accidentally shot merchant Lewis Kissinger in the chest. Dr. McSwegan arrived at the saloon and immediately treated Kissinger. Kissinger's wounds were painful but not deadly. Wilson was immediately arrested and locked in jail until the facts were learned; he was eventually released.

Saloon ads always filled Tombstone's newspapers. Longtime bar keepers Andy Mehan and Thomas Moses, after succumbing to the fire, announced they were now in full blast. They offered a large selection of choice liquors and cigars, and they invited patrons to visit them at Fifth and Fremont. With his business back in full swing, Mehan improved his personal life as he built a "neat cottage" on Fourth Street, between Safford and Bruce.

The Bank Exchange Saloon, which was a popular saloon name in town, was again in business. James Colp and Roderick McNeil purchased a business license to operate their saloon from July to September. The saloon was situated in Tribolet's block on Allen, between Fourth and Fifth streets. They offered the best liquors and cigars, as well as pool and billiard tables, along with cardrooms for those "wishing amusement."

Many frequented the Oriental Saloon, so it's not surprising how many "incidents" took place there. It was on Tuesday morning, November 14, 1882, around seven o'clock, that trouble began. "Buckskin" Frank Leslie and some of his friends were conversing in the Oriental, when William Claiborne, alias "Billy the Kid," entered.[71] According to Leslie and others who testified, Claiborne began using very abusive language to Frank and his friends. Billy also made a comment to Frank and his friends about Dave Neagle. The men warned Billy they were not discussing politics and to leave them. Frank said, "Billy, don't interfere. Those people are friends among themselves and are not talking about politics at all and don't want you about." Frank saw Billy was becoming more offensive, so he escorted him out of the saloon by the coat collar. He advised Billy not to get angry, that it was for his own good, and if he acted in that manner, he was liable to get into trouble.

At that point Billy pointed his finger at Frank and threatened, "That's all right Leslie, I'll get even on you," and stormed off. Not long after, Frank received two different warnings from people advising that Claiborne was waiting outside with his Winchester. Frank went to the Fifth Street entrance of the Oriental and saw Billy with his rifle. Leslie stepped into the street and said, "Billy, don't shoot; I don't want you to kill me, nor I don't want to have to shoot you." As Frank's final words reached Billy's ears, he fired at Frank. He missed, and Frank shot his pistol, striking Billy in the left side of his chest.

By that time, police officer Coyle had arrived on the scene. He immediately disarmed Leslie and arrested him. Claiborne was taken to Dr. Willis's office, where he received treatment. Even though Claiborne was conscious and talking, the doctor could not find Billy's pulse. Billy left of his own accord but later died. Leslie was acquitted, as the coroner's verdict said he acted in self-defense. Tombstone resident and diarist George Parsons wrote, "Frank got the drop on him, being quick as lightning and used to killing men, and the Kid has gone to hell. I say so because, if such a place exists and is for bad men, he is there, as he was a notoriously bad egg and has innocent blood on his head. I *state facts* . . . Frank didn't lose the light of his cigarette during the encounter. Wonderfully cool man."[72]

As if Leslie didn't have enough problems in his life, his mining partner, Joseph Pascholy, was suing him. It seems Leslie owed Pascholy one hundred dollars for work done on their Case Ace Lode mining claim. Leslie had ninety days to pay Pascholy the money or lose his interest in the mine.

As the year 1882 reached its final month, some Tombstone residents decided to have an old-fashioned duel. An altercation between "Bud" Marsh and a man known only as "Cheesey Charley" took place at the Alhambra Saloon. However, before they did any serious damage, Officer Solon arrived and intervened. The two decided to meet the next day to settle their differences. After arming themselves with .45s, the men and their many spectators proceeded to the designated location just outside town. Words were exchanged, and one man said nothing but blood would be spilled. In unusual proceedings, one man remarked that it was a devilishly cold day. The other concluded that a good stiff cocktail "wouldn't be bad to take about this time." The rest of the crowd heartily agreed, so they all went back to town and paid their favorite saloon a visit. After several rounds of drinks, they realized it was too late in the day to fight a duel. One of them remarked,

"According to the Arizona code, affairs of this kind should come off in the cool of the morning."[73] The duel was indefinitely postponed.

With all the recent excitement at the Oriental, its owner, Milton Joyce, decided to visit his ranch in Sulphur Spring Valley, where he had one hundred head of cattle. About the same time, a stone walkway between the Oriental and the Crystal Palace was completed.

While Joyce was at his ranch, the Oriental Saloon was again host to some mischief, but this time no one really got hurt. An old man of about seventy years sat in the back of the saloon near the stove. He slowly worked his way to the bar and said to the barkeeper, "Boss, I think I'll go home, but I'd like a drop of the flush come-to-my-face-quick before I go." Since the barkeeper disliked tramps almost as much as he did old men, he obliged, settling on the lesser of the two evils. After the bartender set out the bottle, the old man took a drink that "would paralyze an army mule." He stood at the bar for a few minutes, and then made his way to the door.

A few minutes later, and unbeknownst to the bartender, he returned to the saloon by way of its rear entrance. He took his previous seat by the stove and after a short time, arose, turned up his collar, and pulled his hat over his eyes. He said to the barkeeper, "Well, I think I'll take a drink and go home; I feel somewhat exhausted from a long walk from Benson." The barkeeper replied, "All right. Pass in your checks, and I'll give you your change." "Well, my boy," said the tramp, "I'm an old man and a poor man and was in hopes you might give me a nightcap." As the barkeeper placed the bottle on the bar, he said, "You look wonderfully like an old tramp I treated a few minutes ago." The old codger replied, "Oh, no, I guess it was my brother." He took his drink and went on his way.

A few moments later the bartender noticed the old tramp back in his seat near the stove, except this time he was wearing an old handkerchief around his neck, his hat tipped to one side, and his coat lapels opened. As he sauntered to the bar for another free drink, the bartender said, "Now look here, my ancient sardine, I'm getting onto to your little game, and it won't go. I've treated you twice within the last half an hour." "Oh, no," replied the tramp, "I think it must have been my brother." The barkeeper replied, "Well, just step outside and fetch them all in; I never hurt a man in my life, but I'll be damned if I wouldn't like to start in and make a clean sweep of a whole family." As he reached under the bar for his club, the old vagrant scooted out the door, perhaps to look for his "brother."[74]

HARRY JOHNSON'S STYLE OF STRAINING MIXED DRINKS
TO A PARTY OF SIX.
Copyrighted, 1888.

Bartender, *Harry Johnson's Bartender's Guide*, 1882, from the author's collection.

Some people, in their quest for a good time, exceeded their limits. One December evening, John Harris and James Carruthers were drinking in Billy Smith's Dexter Saloon. The men were having a discussion, which led to an argument, and neither could arrive at an understanding. To settle their disagreement, the men took to the street where they proposed to fight it out in "true ring style." Several blows were exchanged before Chief Neagle and Officer Solon arrived and hauled the two off to jail. They were booked on a charge of fighting and given bail of twenty dollars. After their court appearance the next day, each man pled guilty and was fined $7.50 plus court costs.

Later that night, and not long after dealing with Harris and Carruthers, Officer Solon was called to Walker's Saloon. Irish miner Edward Gillespie was drinking in the saloon around midnight when he decided to break all of its glassware. By the time Officer Solon

Robert S. Hatch's saloon business license, 1888, courtesy of the Arizona Historical Society.

arrived at the saloon, Gillespie had succeeded in breaking every piece of glassware George Walker had in his saloon. After fighting with the officer, Gillespie was arrested and taken to the city jail.

The end of 1882 brought the close of one of Tombstone's most notable businesses. Pioneer saloon men Robert Hatch and John Campbell called it quits. They dissolved their saloon business and sold all its stock on December 21, 1882. Hatch eventually went on to become deputy sheriff in Tombstone, and later, went back into the saloon business.

1883

Unlike what one might expect in a mining town, many of Tombstone's 1883 saloons were elegant edifices. Local businessmen went to smoke a cigar, have a drink, and discuss politics. In addition to saloons and dance halls, Tombstone had retail and wholesale liquor stores, and breweries. There was the Arizona Brewery operated by Hermann Leptien, the Golden Eagle Brewery on the corner of Seventh and Allen Streets, run by Swiss immigrant Sigfried Tribolet, and the Crystal Palace Saloon, run by Bernhardt Wehrfritz. The Crystal Palace had a restaurant associated with it, the Crystal Palace Chop House. Paul Neunkirch and German baker Hermann Golles owned it. In addition to the restaurant, Wehrfritz offered his patrons entertainment at his adjoining Crystal Palace Theatre.

McClaren and Regant's saloon was on Allen street, opposite the Bird Cage, where they advertised they had the coziest and best stocked establishment in Tombstone. An elegant clubroom with billiard and pool tables was just one of the attractions. Willow Springs, sour mash, Linwood rye, and old bourbon whiskies were always on hand by the barrel, bottle, or glass.

For most businesses in Tombstone, locations changed, as did partners. The longtime partnership of Thomas Moses and Andrew Mehan had come to an end. It was on February 23, 1883 when they dissolved their saloon business known as the Capitol Saloon. Thomas Moses remained at the saloon, while Mehan went to Russelville hoping to find new prospects. By the end of the year, Moses lost his saloon to James Clark in mining title disputes. Billy Smith moved his saloon from Dexter's stable to the room under Schieffelin Hall, previously known as the New York Variety store. Billy's old Dexter Saloon was immediately put up for rent. He named his new saloon the Opera. Before owning his own saloons, Billy tended bar for Andy Robertson and was known as the "well-known mixer" assisting at the bar.

By February the Oriental Saloon was under new ownership. Its proprietor was Richard Heitchow. He took advantage of the saloon's past reputation and advertised "the finest and most popular place of resort in the Territory."[75] He also stated all games were conducted in a strict and respectable manner, and music was provided nightly. Harry Queen's Saloon still graced Allen Street, where the best bit cigar could be had. By March 1884, Harry had moved to Charleston, where he ran a saloon. Lynch & O'Neil also dissolved their partnership; David Lynch retained the business. His new business, simply called Billiard Hall, was on Allen Street, between Fourth and Fifth streets.

James Brophy and George Walker co-owned 521 and 523 Allen Street, where Brophy operated a drinking saloon and Walker had a cigar stand. On February 21, 1883, Brophy sold the property to George Walker for twenty-five hundred dollars and bought a ranch in Sulphur Springs Valley. In July Walker and other parties sold a ranch situated at the base of the Mule Mountains to R. B. Clark for $750. In October, Michael J. Brophy purchased the saloon property from Walker for twenty-five hundred dollars. When Brophy purchased it, Costello and Sullivan ran the drinking saloon. By late November, Walker had closed his cigar store. His store fixtures were

Martin Costello's saloon, 1880s, reproduced by permission of the Arizona Historical Society.

sold to Fielding Brown, who enlarged his cigar store in the Crystal Palace building.

With the Fourth of July barely behind them, Tombstone was stunned by a cyclone on July 6. This cyclone was reported as the most violent storm Tombstone had ever witnessed. It filled the air with debris and huge clouds of dust, and many outbuildings were torn down. As the wind slowly died down, hail, wind, lightning, and rain pounded the city. This storm lasted for about an hour, and then only gentle rain fell upon Tombstone. There were a few structural casualties, but no one was seriously injured. The porch of the San Jose House was torn down and laid on the sidewalk. The cellar of City Hall was flooded, and the signs on the O.K. Corral and the Occidental Restaurant were carried away.

As the city weathered the effects of the cyclone, most residents remained indoors, and some even had parties. At the Senate Saloon several of Tombstone's businessmen gathered to honor attorney Webster Street. He had successfully represented Mayor Carr in a case, so mutual friends gathered to show their appreciation for Street's legal prowess. Street was asked to enter the rear of the saloon by one of his friends, under the guise of asking for legal advice. Once in the back, they began talking about the law, and unbeknownst to Street, men began entering the room in single file, until it was full, and he was surrounded. One of Tombstone's councilmen, Atchison, stepped forward and asked if Street were present. Not quite sure why he was surrounded, Street replied, "Yes." Atchison then asked Street to step forward, which he did. He was then given a lengthy speech about how good a lawyer he was and how thankful everyone was that he had done the mayor justice. At the close of the speech, Street was presented with a handsome walking stick, and he was considered "caned" by the *Republican*. Applause followed the speaker's remarks, during which Street stood in astonishment, completely surprised. The evening ended with endless bottles of champagne being emptied. Speech after speech was made.

The Oriental Saloon, one of Tombstone's most patronized, had lost one of its prime attractions in 1883—Emma Howe—and was in a bind. Not wanting to be without entertainment, the Oriental hired a new singer and pianist named Alice Cook. She made her debut in early July and gave a satisfactory performance. However, the *Republican* said, "As a pianist she far exceeds Miss Emma, and although she has a very good voice, it can hardly be said to equal that of the absent 'nightingale.'"[76]

The *Republican* ran a story it picked up from the *Santa Cruz Sentinel* in late July. "M. E. Joyce, for ten years a resident of Half Moon Bay, San Mateo County, is in Santa Cruz the present week. He is now a resident of Tombstone, Arizona. During the past seven years he has had quite an experience—he has been a businessman, stockbroker, journalist, chairman, board of supervisor, farmer, and cattle raiser. At one time he was reduced to $80; at another time he had $54,000 in bank [*sic*]. At the present date he owns the newspaper *Epitaph*, a cattle range, and cattle."[77] Ironically, Joyce leased the saloon of the Baldwin Theater in San Francisco in August. It was this theater's bar Joyce had purchased back in 1881 for the Oriental. Former Tombstone saloon owner James Vizina was also at the Baldwin with Joyce, where he managed the billiard hall. Three years later, Joyce lived in San Francisco full-time when his wife presented him with a baby boy on February 28.

Billy Smith's new Opera Saloon, located under Schieffelin Hall, celebrated a grand opening on the night of October 5, 1883. One of

Tombstone's veteran caterers, Charley Brickwedel, prepared a temping light fare for Billy's guests to sample while they enjoyed the sounds of a musical band. Billy's saloon also offered billiard tables to add to the pleasure of the environment.

Just as Billy Smith's new saloon opened, for the first time the city of Tombstone had gas illumination and no longer had to use dirty coal oil. A contract between the city and the gas light company was finally signed in early October. It ordered the company to erect and maintain twenty street lamps, with iron posts, along the mains of the gas company. They were also required to keep the lamps lit from sundown to sunrise when the moon was less than half full and on cloudy moonlit nights. They were required to light and extinguish the lamps at their own expense and furnish burners. The lights were not less than sixteen candle power, and the cost was five dollars per month.

Despite some feelings of "doom," many in Tombstone remained optimistic about its outlook. With the addition of the gasworks and a new school building, Tombstone boasted it was the best supplied town in Arizona when it came to buildings and improvements. It had a fine courthouse, city hall, a large theater building and two buildings fitted for variety shows, Turn Verein hall, four churches, two schoolhouses, splendid waterworks, and a well maintained and equipped fire department. The *Republican* reported that businessmen expressed a greater feeling of confidence than had been felt for some months past.

David Lynch apparently didn't look upon Tombstone as optimistically as the *Republican* did. In late October 1883, he closed his saloon in Tombstone and packed up for Bisbee, where he opened a saloon. Lynch's saloon did not work out, and eventually he went to work for another old Tombstoner named Patrick Coffee. Coffee had acquired a new saloon in Bisbee from Sol Pierce earlier in May.

The Oriental saloon's one-time owners, Benjamin Cook and James Vizina parted ways in January 1883, when Vizina sold half of the building to Cook to settle his debts. As noted earlier, Vizina was now in San Francisco working for Milt Joyce. Cook continued to own the building but did not run the saloon. In October, the Oriental Saloon and clubhouse was being run by Bagby and Speck, who advertised their saloon had a private wine room and offered nightly music. However, while the proprietors were celebrating success, an unfortunate incident took place. At 7:30 p.m. on October 30, a large crowd hastily collected to see what had happened. After hearing several crackling noises, a twenty-foot section of the Oriental's Saloon wall came crashing down onto Fifth Street.

Fortunately, no one was injured. Apparently the Huachuca Water Company had made a hole in the wall, to allow the pipes to enter the building. Making a hole in the adobe had weakened it, and standing water from an inside public faucet and drinking tank dampened the walls and rotted them until they finally gave out. The owner of the building, Benjamin Cook, immediately hired men to repair the damage and rebuild the wall.

With gas lighting the city of Tombstone glowed with illumination for the first time, and just in time for Thanksgiving. The Tombstone Gas Company had begun supplying the city with lights, and the Oriental, Crystal Palace, and many other businesses sparkled with new lighting. By December, Tombstone was shining brightly and shimmering with wealth. Christmas was especially nice in town that year, and the restaurants, saloons, and gambling houses were more liberally patronized than usual. The total amount of revenue collected from saloons, wine rooms, and liquor dealers was $1,657.35, and $1,300 was collected on gambling tables and games, such as faro, monte, and twenty-one.[78] Numerous strangers were seen on the streets who had come into town from the rural districts. There was even a horse race at Doling's track.

1884

William A. Cuddy, former Tombstone resident and bartender, had moved to Phoenix in 1883 and took up the occupation of attorney. The *Republican* printed a quote from the *Phenix* [sic] *Gazette* on January 19, 1884, regarding Cuddy. "Counselor Cuddy made his debut in the courts of this city yesterday, appearing as a prosecuting attorney in a criminal trial before Justice Morris. The counselor, it is unnecessary to state, has never been admitted to any bar, outside of those who supply 'wet groceries' to the public." In 1885 "Counselor" Cuddy moved to Modesto, California. Once in Modesto, he secured employment from Albert Bilicke, who owned the Cosmopolitan Hotel in Tombstone before the second fire. Cuddy was in charge of the entire operation until he let the whiskey manage the business for him. He and Bilicke had words, and he departed. He then went on a drinking binge in Stockton. While intoxicated, Cuddy and some friends stumbled upon a group of men and women preaching the gospel of the Lord. It wasn't long after that when Cuddy himself became reformed and renounced alcohol, tobacco, gambling, swearing, dance halls, and shows.[79] In 1886 he married Henrietta Piccott in San Luis Obispo, California.

Once again, dust had become public enemy number one in Tombstone. By early 1884, citizens and merchants alike complained about the dusty conditions. They urged the city council to buy water that was pumped out from the mines and sprinkle the streets. If the city council did this, residents could walk about town without appearing as if they had ridden the range for days, and merchants could place goods and bins on their sidewalks.

Tombstone's saloons offered a huge variety of items, and most supplied beverages typically available only in their saloon. The Crystal Palace Saloon offered six-year-old, double-stamp Hermitage whiskey as well as Key West cigars. The Occidental Wine House, which opened in February 1884 in the Occidental Hotel Building, offered the best brands of French wines and California wines. The Fountain Saloon under the old Grand Hotel offered imported Baltimore oysters and the finest imported lunches. Oysters were served in all styles. Oysters were also offered at the Boca Saloon on Allen Street. They sold Boca beer and offered clam chowder and domestic and imported lunches.

The Union Soda Works, under the ownership of Frederick Blush from early 1881 until February 11, 1884, sold half his interest to Charles A. Buddington for one dollar. The transaction included the business, one house and lot fronting Toughnut Street, all the machinery, three horses, and two wagons. A year later, Blush sold the other half of the business to Buddington for five dollars.

The Crystal Palace Saloon was one of a few saloons that had a female faro dealer. Former Tombstone resident, John Hancock reminisced about seeing her in Tombstone in the 1880s.[80] He said

One of the best faro dealers I ever saw was a girl that used to deal sometimes on afternoons for a gambler that went by the name of 'Napa Nick' who had a faro bank in the old Crystal Palace Saloon.[81] She was a handsome girl about 21 or 22 years of age and had evidently come from a good family. There was nothing harsh or coarse about her and she was always well-dressed in the prevailing styles but not loud or gaudy, and her diamonds were always appropriate and while they lent their charm to her beauty they were not out of place or seemed to have been put on for show; and the way she could deal faro was a revelation to any old-timer that thought he was pretty slick at the game. Often in an idle moment while the players were deciding on how to place their bets, she would 'shuffle a stack of chips,' that is, she would take a stack of chips and divide it in two equal stacks and place one beside the other, then by manipulation of her forefinger and thumb she would raise the chips on edge without removing them entirely from the table, and let them slip through her fingers in such a manner so that the chips would fall on top of the other in rotation, if two chips happened to fall instead of one then it was not perfect; many a time I have watched her but she never made a mistake—she was absolutely perfect. The dealer in those days was considered an apprentice until he could shuffle a stack of chips with an unconscious detachment—absentmindedly as it were."

Once a partner in that saloon, Sigfried Tribolet was doing well at his own business—the Golden Eagle Brewery. While it continued to be a popular resort in town, Tribolet also kept a "depot" brewery in nearby Bisbee. He sold his beer at the wholesale rates of fifty cents per gallon or two dollars per dozen for bottled beer; it was delivered free of charge. The Golden Eagle also tempted customers by offering free lunch. Tribolet announced his brewery was the largest in the territory, at least according to the Internal Revenue Bureau. Tribolet's income must have exceeded two thousand dollars per year, because according to the 1870 Tax Act, anyone exceeding that amount must file a tax return. The tax act required all income to be claimed, even that earned by a minor child and wife. Anyone having gold on hand had to calculate its value based on its worth at the end of the tax year. Completed tax forms were submitted to the assistant assessor in one's district by March 1 of the following tax year.

An item near and dear to the Golden Eagle Brewery, as well as many other businesses in town, was ice. While some places in and nearby Tombstone made ice, Fred W. Smith offered imported Rocky Mountain Ice. He managed and took orders for the Natural Ice Company in Tombstone.

Saloon owner Anton Hittinger opened his business around August, but quickly moved back to Tucson. He sold his property on Allen Street to tobacco shop owners Adolph and David Cohn for twenty-six thousand dollars on November 11, 1884. Hittinger eventually went to Benson in 1886.

1885

The year 1885 began rather quietly and slowly. Businesses did well, and so did the mines. The weather, although extremely dry, was pleasant.

Check to Anton Hittinger, 1884, from the author's collection.

Residents tended to their daily duties and attended theater performances and balls.

While many businesses opened, closed, and sometimes reopened,
the Crystal Palace, once known as the Golden Eagle, remained steady as
an oak. Its owner, Ben Wehrfritz, had been behind the bar since 1879.
Sigfried Tribolet was once his partner, but after they split, Ben took on no
new partners—until now. On April 4, he sold one-half of his interest in
the Crystal Palace Saloon to Julius Caesar for twenty-five hundred dollars.
The two men became partners and began a successful campaign of selling spirits, as well as ice. Caesar, along with his wife, Sophie, also kept
their New York Restaurant in town.

A letter, supposedly from Geronimo to Caesar and Wehrfritz,
appeared in the *Daily Republican*. The letter began, "Gentlemen: I have
just arrived in the Sierra Madre mountains and hasten to at once
acquaint you with the fact that but for the timely arrival of that shipment of ice cold beer received by me when so hotly pursued by Captains
James and Rafferty, my-self and warrior might inevitably have been taken
in. When the beer was passed around to my braves it put new life into
them, and we immediately took up the double quick for the Sierra
Madres, where we arrived safe and sound. I send by the mail courier
who carries the letter a scalp, which you may hang up in the saloon.
When I have made my treaty with Grey Fox I will call and sample some
of the ice-cold Anheuser and Boca beer kept on draught in the patent
German fountain. I expect to make a treaty and be on my way back to the
reservation in about four months."[82]

German saloon owner Otto Bauer and Daniel O'Connor dissolved
their partnership on August 14 when O'Connor retired. A few months
before he retired from the business, O'Connor was granted United States

citizenship. The store was still called Bauer & O'Connor's, at least for a while, even though Bauer was the sole proprietor. He offered the popular Conqueror Key West cigar, which was manufactured by Soldenburg & Co. A year later, Bauer assigned his Cuba Cigar store to his creditors, who sold it to Adolph Cohn.

W. S. Harmoh tried a different approach when it came to the saloon business. In August 1885, he opened the Casino Gardens. It was situated on Allen Street, between Tenth and Eleventh Streets. He renovated the previous building and welcomed newcomers. In his ad he wrote, "The proprietor of this establishment proposes to make this an evening sport for families. No improper characters will be admitted." In early September, Mrs. Hovey took charge of the Casino Gardens and threw an open invitation ball to celebrate her grand opening. She advertised, "Come and dance and be merry."

The beer, tobacco, and liquor sold in Tombstone were almost as diverse as its population. There was Schlitz Milwaukee beer, sold "ice cold" and on draught at Haeffner & Shaughnesay's Billiard Parlors on Allen Street. Macneil, Moore & Co. were the sole agents in Tombstone for Budweiser beer. The Willows Saloon, next door to the O.K. Corral, was the pride and joy of John F. Crowley and Harry Stevenson. Johnny and Harry sold Cliff Springs bourbon and Tea Kettle rye. They also specialized in fancy mixed drinks of all kinds. Adolph Cohn & Bros. sold meerschaum and amber goods and was the sole agent for the "Slote" cigar. Adolph traveled to New York, as well as California, to procure a vast variety of goods for his store. It was evident beer consumption was up at the St. Louis beer hall on Allen Street, based on the more than eight hundred empty Gambrinus kegs piled up in front of the saloon.

Gus Williams's Tombstone Parlors on Allen Street continuously offered fine mixed drinks and cardrooms. His saloon was popular, but a new item displayed in the bar in late August caused many men to drop in to see it. It was an advertisement from Pomery Sec' Wine Company, and it hung on the saloon's wall. The ad, made of bronze, depicted the corselet of a crusader and portrayed the image of a baron's hall. Gus also reportedly had the best game rooster in town, and kept him on display at the bar. All lovers of the prize ring were encouraged to stop by and see him before his fights.

Andy Mehan had returned to Tombstone six months earlier from Russelville, and his saloon once again gained popularity. Andy's Allen Street saloon even sported a new mirror that was a "daisy." Unfortunately, just as Andy's saloon was on its way to becoming one of the town's most popular resorts, he was arrested, in late August, for assault with a deadly weapon. By mid-September his case had come to trial; after the jury deliberated for just over five hours, the members rendered a verdict of simple assault. Counsel for the defense immediately asked for a new trial, which was granted and set for the following week. Mehan was allowed to leave on his own recognizance after posting a two-hundred-dollar bond. By the early part of 1886, Mehan had sold his saloon to Nathan Leigh and became a constable in town. Leigh's Headquarters Saloon on Allen Street sat opposite the Occidental Hotel. Leigh didn't last very long in Tombstone. By April of the following year, he had left town and was running a trader's store at Mescal Springs in the Whetstone Mountains.

Even though the mines were quiet, the streets of Tombstone were not. Sounds of daily life resonated in Tombstone, and the *Daily Record Epitaph,* whose office was on Fremont Street, noted a different sound. A reporter wrote in the September 5, 1885, paper, "A number of musical voices are located in the immediate vicinity of the . . . office and almost every evening the dulcet strains of 'Wait Till the Clouds Roll By,' 'At Night When the Opera is Over,' and selections from Norms, Fra Diavolo, Lucia de Lommermour, and other favorites are wafted into the sanctum. 'Tis an unexpected pleasure." It was around this same time that the Bank Exchange Saloon bid adieu to Miss Erba Robeson, "whose sweet voice and charm of manner has delighted habituates of the Bank Exchange for some time," according to the *Daily Record Epitaph,* which recorded her departure to Silver City, New Mexico.[83]

The Crystal Palace, still a popular saloon, was the scene of yet another fight on September 5. This time a saloonkeeper named Frank Broad and a miner named Charley Cunningham were the perpetrators. On Saturday, patrons in the saloon saw the fight and said it was "a neat bit of sparring." Both men were hauled off to jail where they were booked for fighting and placed under twenty-dollar bonds until their case could be heard on Monday morning. On Monday, Broad was charged with fighting, but pled not guilty, so a trial by jury was set for later that day. Charley Cunningham's name did not appear on the police record with Broad's.[84]

By the end of the month, Broad was indirectly involved with another fight, this time, at his own saloon on Allen Street just above Fifth. Bisbee's champion fighter, Big Jack, and a couple of "Tombstone's lightweights" got into a good old-fashioned bar brawl. Glasses flew as chairs were crushed on Big Jack's back, which caused him to tumble into the empty beer kegs on the sidewalk. Despite the noise and confusion, no one was injured or arrested. Within a month, Broad was out of business. Broad, however, was destined to remain in the saloon business. By March 1886 he was once again running a saloon, where he offered a free acrobatic performance every afternoon. Broad also joined a troop of men to protect Tombstone from raiding Indians a couple of months later.

Former Oriental Saloon owner Lou Rickabaugh's name appeared in the Tombstone paper around mid-September 1885. While Lou was in his room in the Cosmopolitan Hotel in Tucson, a sporting man from Colorado named William Bennett went to Lou's room with his pistol in hand. He stood in front of Lou's rooms and called for him to come out and fight. Rickabaugh refused and told him to go away. Bennett then told Rickabaugh he would kick the door in and kill him if he didn't come out. With his life being threatened, Rickabaugh opened a side door and stepped out with his pistol. Rickabaugh, who was quicker than Bennett, shot the man in the left knee, which caused him to drop his pistol. He was taken to the hospital with little chance to live. On September 23, 1885, the case was dismissed as the evidence indicated Rickabaugh acted in self-defense.

On September 15, 1885, the *Daily Record Epitaph* published the details of the recently amended ordinance number four. This ordinance was originally approved by the mayor and city council on April 5, 1881. It provided for the licensing of any business or trade being conducted within the city limits. It was a misdemeanor not to have a license, and guilty parties were fined up to one hundred dollars or imprisoned for a maximum of thirty days, or both. The monthly licensing fees were as follows:

Assayers	$ 1.50
Billiard Tables	$ 1.50 (per table)
Breweries	$ 4.00
Circus or Menagerie	$ 12.50 (per day, while in town)
Club rooms	$ 7.00 (where cards and dice were played for drinks)
Hotels (first-class)	$ 6.00 (twenty bed maximum)
Ice	$ 4.00 (selling or delivering)
Pawnbrokers	$ 10.00 (must keep detailed record books)
Ten-Pin Alleys	$ 4.00 (per alley)

Some of the other licensing fees were a bit more complicated. The ordinance read, "The owners or lessee of any house, room, or cellar, where wines, malt, or spirituous liquors are sold by the bottle or glass, where dancing is carried on and generally known as dance houses or cellars shall pay a daily license of two dollars ($2.00) or a monthly license of sixty ($60.00) at the discretion of the person applying for the license."

The license for barrooms matched that of a liquor license, except it applied to every person or firm engaged in keeping a barroom or public saloon. The cost of the license varied depending on the bar's monthly receipts. A first-class license applied to those whose sales were eight hundred dollars or higher and cost seven dollars per month. The monthly fees for second- and third-class licenses varied depending upon the sales.

Gambling licenses were even more complex. The ordinance read, "For each and every person who shall deal, play, or carry on, open or cause to be opened or who shall conduct either as owner or employee whether for hire or not, any game such as Monte, faro, pass faro, Monte rondeau, Roulette, twenty-one, dice, (red and black roughet-noir [sic]), lansquenette, tan, stud horse poker, or keno or any other game banking of whatever name, whether played with cards or dice or any other device shall be played for money, checks, credit or any other valuable thing or representative of value the monthly license fee shall be $10."

The license for shooting galleries varied according to the type of establishment. "Every person or firm engaged in the business of keeping a pistol, gun, or rifle shooting gallery shall pay a monthly license of $3 to carry on the same, provided, however, that no license shall issue unless said gallery be provided with sliding or movable targets or some other device or arrangement by which the markers can call the shots and mark the target or targets without coming in range between them and the place where the person stands shooting."

Houses of ill fame had two types of licensing fees. The first one stated, "Every person or persons or proprietors engaged in keeping a house of ill fame where wines, malts, or spirituous liquors are sold by the glass or bottle shall pay a monthly license fee of $20." If the house of ill fame did not sell liquor, the monthly fee was reduced to seven dollars.

When the amended ordinances were posted in Tombstone, many citizens were panicked and outraged. The city council and the local papers reminded people that the same reaction resulted when the ordinance was first passed in 1881. Once citizens were advised Tombstone's ordinances were similar to those in Virginia City and Los Angeles, their fears quieted.

With the variety of saloons and drinking houses in town, businessmen and women had to be creative to entice customers to try their saloon over the competition's. The *Daily Record Epitaph* printed an interesting note about John Shaughnesay of the Billiard Parlor Saloon. "'The way to a man's heart is through his stomach,' is an old and trite saying, but it does not wholly apply to [?]. Drink to those who appreciate fine liquors, artificially served, is a condiment not to be overlooked, and few among the many mixologists of Tombstone can cater to the wants of the bibulous as can John Shaughnesay."[85] Shaughnesay also attracted customers by displaying a peanut plant with peanuts, roots, and vines. The plant was a gift from the Tombstone Milling & Mining Company's manager, George Cheyney, who grew the plant in his garden in the lush soil along the San Pedro River. Shaughnesay, his partner Haeffner, Martin Costello, and Gilbert S. Bradshaw placed a notice in the paper stating they intended to sell beer at $5.50 per keg and would deliver twenty pounds of ice for free until further notice.

The Crystal Palace Saloon owners, Wehrfritz and Caesar, constructed a patent refrigerator for storing beer. It stood sixteen feet high and was divided by an iron floor into two compartments. The lower part, for beer, was six feet tall and held over one carload of kegs. The space above was large enough to hold a couple of carloads of ice. Within three or four days, Tombstone residents were enjoying ice-cold beer direct from St. Louis breweries. They also sold ice at two and one-half cents per pound to anyone and everyone.

Benjamin Cook, who owned the Oriental Saloon building at the corner of Fifth and Allen Streets, announced this newly renovated building was available for rent. Two months later, longtime saloon man Joseph "Charley" Mellgren was at the helm. Local contractors were hired to renovate the saloon, and he ordered a new bar and fixtures from a company in Chicago. The paper said, "It would indicate that Ben is expecting a little boom for Tombstone." Ben continued to prosper and never gave up hope on Tombstone and its future. He remained there until he passed away on October 30, 1915. He left his estate to his two daughters, Willette Lorraine and Frances Rebecca. It included 33,350 shares of Herschell mining stock, six Bear Valley Water

J. L. Mellgren, courtesy of his grandson, Dr. Walter Mellgren.

bonds, Greene Cananea stock, and one thousand shares of Commonwealth Extension mining stock. He also left his four-room frame house on Third Street and a rental property at the corner of Bruce and Fourth.

Ben Wehrfritz and Julius Caesar once again published a "letter from Geronimo" in the *Daily Tombstone* on November 17, 1885. It was entitled, "Not Dead." It read, "Sierra Madres. August 27, 1885. Messrs. Caesar and Wehrfritz: see by late copies of the *Tombstone* that I was reported seriously wounded and it was thought I would die. These reports are not correct, as I am not wounded nor am I dead, but I tell you that I am awful dry, and I want you to send me a consignment of that ice cold Anheuser beer, that you are selling to the people of Tombstone. I only wish I was there to have it drawn from that German patent fountain. Geronimo."

1886

Caesar and Wehrfritz may have thought using Geronimo for advertising was clever, but the threat of his depredations was real. So real, in fact, that Cochise County Sheriff Bob Hatch placed a reward on his head. In the early part of January 1886, Hatch ran a newspaper ad that read

> $500 Reward. By virtue of the authority vested in me by the Board of Supervisors of Cochise County at a regular meeting of said Board, held on the 6th day of October, 1885, I hereby offer a reward of $500 for the apprehension, dead or alive, of the renegade Apache Chief Geronimo. And by the same authority, I offer a further reward of $250 for the apprehension, dead or alive, of any one of said Geronimo's band of renegade Indians who have been engaged with him in his murderous raids through Cochise County. Such apprehension, to earn the above rewards, must be made by some person or persons not in the military service of the United States.[86]

Oriental owner and bartender Joseph "Charley" Mellgren was also creative in advertising. In response to early 1886 ads in the newspapers that proper Victorian ladies placed to receive callers, he placed this ad: "Charles Mellgren will receive callers all day long tomorrow at the Oriental."[87] Charley was a character in his own right and was well liked by the *Daily Tombstone* newspaper. The paper wrote, "There is only one man in Tombstone and in the world that can mix drinks. There used to be two, Charley Mellgren, and a man in Boston. But the man in Boston died, and Charley Mellgren of the Oriental Saloon is the boss." The paper's next paragraph read, "Talk about fine looking men, if you want to see a good looking man go to the Oriental Saloon and gaze upon Chas. Mellgren, and then turn your attention to the hand-somest woman in the world and the sweetest singer in the world." Miss Jennings was the singer to whom the ad referred. To add to his customers' enjoyment, Charley offered a variety of liquors and cigars, including A. A. Bourbon; Cyrus Noble's white rye, ale, and porter; Baldwin, Nagle, and Martel brandies; imported ports and sherry; and Holland gin. Available cigars were Estrella and Operatas. Charley's motto was, "Quick sales and small profits."[88] Mellgren had been an early Tombstonian, and was once proprietor of the noted Alhambra Saloon. Another example of Mellgren's advertising ingenuity was his recurring advertisement that closely resembled the items published by the board of supervisors. It was titled "Annual Meeting of Cowboys and Miners of Cochise County." It stated

> At the regular meeting of the cowboys and miners of Cochise County held in this city on January 1, 1886, the following resolution and preamble was adopted: Whereas, Since our last meeting at the Oriental, under the management of J. L. Mellgren, has become one of the substantial houses of the city. Therefore, be it resolved, that for the year 1886, the Oriental is hereby designated as the place where we shall assemble and congregate, every day and night during the year. As the vote was about to be taken, Mr. Patrick Jeremiah O'Houlahan, one of the valued members of the society, arose and asked the object of resolution and what they should go there for? The President, Mr. Fritz Van Doozle Schummerhorn, stated that it was to get the finest wines, liquors and cigars, and the best of mixed drinks. On motion, the resolution was adopted and the Oriental was declared to be the official headquarters of the Association, and that J. L. Mellgren be ordered to be always present to minister the wants of members.[89]

A few days later, he advertised Boston baked beans and roast beef were on the menu for lunch at nine o'clock in the evening. In addition to owning and managing a successful saloon, Mellgren was the Select Commander for the Ancient Order of United Workmen. He was honored at the latest meeting held by the order, for his work for 1885. Since Mellgren was retiring, member Benjamin Goodrich stepped up on the stage and asked Mellgren to join him. Once Mellgren was on the stage, Goodrich presented him with a gold locket as the Order's token of their regard and esteem. Mellgren said he "hoped that he would always retain the esteem and respect of his fellow members."[90]

At the beginning of 1886, the *Daily Tombstone* newspaper took some time to look at who the major players were in the business world about town. They noted Gus Williams's saloon was a popular resort in Tombstone and few passed his door without stopping in. Gus said he was getting old and feeble, but the paper said he was still in the ring.[91] By mid-January, Charles H. Mauk had purchased Gus's saloon. Charlie, who retained the name of the saloon, offered spiced beef tea and other choice liquors and cigars. He also offered an attached cardroom for patrons. The *Daily Tombstone* said, "Chas. is the boss mixologist in town."[92]

ROBERT S. HATCH, Sheriff.   CHAS. D. REPPY, Under Sheriff.

⊹ OFFICE OF ⊹

✤ SHERIFF COCHISE COUNTY. ✤

Tombstone, Arizona, May 3 *1886*

To A. J. Ritter
          County Treasurer
   Sir —
          Herewith I hand you Three Hundred and
Sixty-two and ⁶⁵/₁₀₀ Dollars ($362.⁶⁵) moneys
collected by me during the month ending April 30,
1886, from the following sources, viz:
          From Gambling Licenses $ 25.00
             "   Other   "   207.00
             "   Fees   116.65
             "   Fines   14.00
                                              $362.65

                              R. S. Hatch, Sheriff,
                          By C. D. Reppy
                                       Under Sheriff;

Tombstone's gambling license fees collected for April 1886, courtesy of the Arizona Historical Society.

The Crystal Palace Saloon, still owned by Julius Caesar and Bernhardt Wehrfritz, was one of the most popular saloons in town. The Palace not only brewed its own beer, but kept a well stocked bar. A patron could choose to "buck the tiger" or listen to sweet singing and beautiful music by an accomplished musician. Patrons of the Crystal Palace were treated to a special performance by the "Little German Silver Coronet and Catgut String Band." This popular band had performed for the crowned heads of Europe and the elite of the United States. Stopping in Tombstone, they gave their performance at eleven o'clock on the evening of January 1, 1886. Wehrfritz and Caesar provided complimentary beer, sauerkraut, and pretzels to all that attended. In addition to the bar food served at the Crystal Palace, there was a restaurant attached. There was a separate entrance to Fred Parker's Crystal Palace Lunch Parlors on Fifth Street. His offerings included sandwiches, hot lunches, and oysters served in all styles. Meals at the lunch parlors cost two bits and up.

Campbell's Keg House was the newest "resort" on the saloon circuit. Henry Campbell elaborately adorned his saloon and only sold the finest liquors right from the barrels. Some of his drink specialties included Tom and Jerrys, hot Scotch whiskey, champagne cocktails, fine Old Hermitage bourbon and rye, W. H. McBrayer, Tea Kettle, Gains Private stock whiskeys, and hot Jamaica, St. Croix, and New England rums. He also imported English ale and porter. In July, Henry Campbell sold his Keg House and purchased the Pony Saloon from Thomas Jones. Henry received an elegant beer chest from the East, and cool, superior lager was then dispensed at the Pony. Shortly after taking possession of the Pony in mid-July, Henry suffered from the effects of malaria. Campbell was the third owner of this popular saloon, which was originally established back in 1880 by Fielding C. Brown. Sadly, Tombstone pioneer Brown passed away on September 4, 1886. Thomas Jones, the second owner, sold the saloon to Campbell as he departed for Nogales and his new hotel venture. Like his predecessor, Tom welcomed everyone and offered a good word and a smile.[93]

The Willows Saloon, owned by Harry Stevenson and John F. Crowley, remained one of the coziest places in town, where nothing but choice liquors and cigars were sold. Harry Stevenson and Dick Reynolds were on their way home in a buckboard when their team approached the adobe yards. A large freight team startled their horses, and Harry's team started to run, so he held the reins and got them down to a fast trot. After a few minutes of this the front wheels came off, throwing the men from their buggy. Harry held the reins for a short time longer as the horses dragged him through the streets of Tombstone. Nearing exhaustion, Harry finally let go, and the team raced even farther through town, tearing up Toughnut Street to Sixth and then up to Allen and down toward Contention. They were finally halted when Frank Abbot mounted his horse and stopped them. No one in town knew to whom the horses belonged, until they saw Harry limping into town with his clothes torn and dirty.

The Fashion Saloon was one of the leading establishments in Tombstone. Gilbert S. Bradshaw, a native of Canada, sold nothing but the best liquors and cigars. Tombstone locals often frequented the Fashion in order to enjoy a glass of Milwaukee beer on draught. Since Bradshaw had a robust personality, he had numerous "friends" keeping his saloon busy. The *Daily Tombstone* said the Fashion Saloon was the boss place for beef tea. Bradshaw hung two photos of the winning Rescue Hose Company in his saloon.

The Elite Saloon, owned by Ege Ashmun and Walker, rang in the new year by offering eggnog. Their saloon also offered patrons billiard tables, pool tables, and cardrooms. People were asked to stop by and see the new sign painted on the mirror behind the bar. The saloon also made a

Long John. Tall gentleman in elegant
suit sitting and enjoying his cigar in
a Victorian chair, which is tilting back
at a precarious angel. Black and
white lithograph 1870. Circular
composition, four tiny vignettes in the
corners
1870.

Long John cigar ad, from the
author's collection.

special point of carrying the popular and celebrated Old Forrester
whiskey and new Jockey Queen cigars. Albert Fortlouis, one of
Tombstone's pioneer businessmen, remained a force to be reckoned with
in town. Although he did not compete with the saloons in town, he did
sell liquor, wine, brandy, cordials, and cigars to the wholesale market, the
camps scattered around the territory, and the Sonora market. Fortlouis's
private life was also going well. He was a newlywed in town, having married Miss Heyman in November of the previous year. Albert bought the
old Stanton ranch from Ben James just prior to his wedding, where he
and his bride lived. Not letting marriage interfere with his business,
Albert filed a complaint against H. Vandenburg for not paying his bill of
$153.20. Vandenburg was required to pay his debt or appear in court next
year, on January 6, 1886. Despite their success, Ashmun and Walker sold
their saloon and all its fixtures in late January to Albert Fortlouis.
Fortlouis hired Gus Williams, who had just sold his saloon, to manage the
bar. Fortlouis then sold the Elite's bar fixtures. By April though, Ashmun
and Walker were back in business together at the Tobacco Emporium.
They sold the new handmade Havana Cuba cigar and genuine plug
tobacco with the seal of North Carolina. They also offered Lorillard's new
cognac chewing tobacco. Two months later, they sold their tobacco business to a commercial traveler named Gus Heyman.

Shaughnesay and Haeffner, who owned the billiard parlors opposite the old Grand Hotel building, entertained a lucrative crowd every
night. Their establishment was said to be the oldest in the city, and
they offered their customers pool tables, billiard tables, and card
tables. They also installed an ice chest and offered Schlitz Milwaukee
beer. They hired Johnny Noble to tend their bar, but in July he left for
the hot springs in Arkansas for his health. Noble returned to
Tombstone, but eventually quit the saloon business to work with his
brother at his fruit and vegetable stand.

Milwaukee beer was popular in Tombstone, but apparently not
enough to keep the sales up. A report published in 1886 showed the
statistics of Milwaukee beer production. Sales figures from 1885 were
compared to those from 1884. Joseph Schlitz's brewery only produced
317,408 barrels in 1885, as opposed to 339,103 barrels in 1884. Val Blatz's
brewery, however, increased its production from about 135,143 barrels
in 1884 compared to 145,000 in 1885. Overall, there was a decrease of
32,145 barrels from all Milwaukee brewers in 1885.[94]

New to the liquor scene in January 1886 were G. M. Dallas &
Brother at 505 Allen Street. They received a large stock of supplies said
to be valued at thirty thousand dollars. The stock included whiskeys,
fruit brandies, cordials, creams, extracts, and bitters. They also
received American, German, French, and Swedish liquors, ryes, bour-
bons, gins, ports, and rums. They advertised, "Jobbers of bar fixtures
and cards. We respectfully solicit family trade and have in cases 6 to 12
bottles."[95] Six months later, on June 11, George and his brother Charles
sold their business to Louis Van Burt and then left for Chicago.

One late January afternoon, two miners got into a dispute at
Leptien's Saloon on Allen Street. The doors of the saloon were closed,
and the men were allowed to fight it out. After thumping each other
sufficiently, they both became tired, and the fight was called a draw.
Hermann Leptien's popular saloon received a large shipment of very
choice morsels for his lunch "larder." He also kept Lemp's celebrated
beer on tap and received large shipments of ice from California. Eight
months later, Hermann and his wife told their friends they were
returning to the homeland. Upon hearing the news, their friends held
a party for them at city hall's banquet room. The *Daily Tombstone*
wrote, "The earliest settlers know him and many a tired and worn out
prospector has blessed him for a schooner of his home brewed beer,
an article that Mr. Leptien has but few equals in making. Mr.
Leptien was the first man to introduce schooners, and brewed his

own beer up to the present year when imported beer could be laid down in Tombstone cheaper than malt and hops. He then introduced P. Weiland's beer and kept it on hand until he made up his mind to go to his old home in Germany."[96]

Tombstone, like any other town, kept up with all the latest trends, whether it was fashion or drinking. Beef tea had once again become all the rage in early 1886. The *Daily Tombstone* reported saloons were pondering whether or not they should offer ham and eggs with their beef tea, beginning the first of the month. Gus Williams, owner of Elite Saloon, offered all the popular drinks of the time, including beef tea, hot scotch, and chicken broth.

In late February 1886, the Fashion Saloon's patrons were able to gaze at the stars from inside the saloon. Its owner, Gilbert Bradshaw, had installed a new skylight during renovations. He also included a new reading room filled with the current papers and periodicals of the time and "fitted up" some handsome cardrooms. Bradshaw's Fashion Saloon also employed W. A. McAllister, one of Tombstone's best mixologists. Bradshaw was president of the Tombstone Rescue Hose Company and otherwise involved in the community. He offered a prize to the little girl who sold the most tickets to a Tombstone Dramatic Club's evening benefit. The proceeds benefited Tombstone's cemetery fund. When Bradshaw wasn't busy with his saloon or fighting fires in town, he went hunting in the mountains with his friends.

In March of 1886, the anti-Chinese movement heated up in Tombstone, and many of Tombstone's prominent citizens took part. Saloonkeepers Joseph Mellgren, Shaughnesay & Haeffner, Charles Mauk, and Gilbert S. Bradshaw were business owners who had recently discharged their Chinese help. As a token of appreciation, the anti-Chinese movement sent the Elite Theatre's brass band to serenade them, as they made their way to the next meeting at Schieffelin Hall to discuss the Chinese problem. Once the music ended, attendees heard speeches from various individuals. Judge Robinson, who suffered from a bad cold, gave the main speech. Despite his illness and hoarse voice, Robinson's message was clear—the Chinese must be stopped! He stated the Chinese had overrun San Francisco, and if they weren't careful, Tombstone would be next. He said it was the citizens' duty not to hire them, nor patronize any business where Chinese were employed. He said he wanted to rid Tombstone of the Chinese, but did not believe in violence of any kind.

Saying he was too hoarse to finish, he asked dairy farmer Carlisle S. Abbott to continue. Abbott said, "There is not much use in discussing this question, as it was the white race on one side, who raised families, supported government, built churches and public schools and who were the sovereign people of these United States, any one of whom is worth forty Chinamen. And the pig tails, on the other hand supported the Chinese Empire, did not support our government, built no churches or schools, and who had such a love for their own country and such a hatred for ours that they would not even let their bones remain in this country after their death."[97] He asked the townspeople to band together and refuse them employment and refuse to patronize those who hired them.

Judge Riley was then asked to step forward and give his comments. The Judge stated he did not give long speeches, but said a few words anyway. Riley claimed the whites were as much to blame as the Chinese. He said, "We must first reform ourselves. Upstarts, who had suddenly grown rich, wanted flunkeys to wait on them. White labor was too independent for them. Then, again, as they were ignorant, as was often the case, they feared their white servants might despise them. The shoddy aristocracy of this country are as much to blame for the growth of this Chinese evil."[98] More speeches were made, and the meeting ended.

Joseph Mellgren continued to fill the papers with his advertisements, especially after the anti-Chinese movement began. Because he did not immediately discharge his Chinese help at the onset of the movement, many boycotted his saloon. The Oriental Saloon was one of a few saloons that kept its Chinese help. Unfortunately, after the pressure of slow sales and harassment from townspeople, Mellgren fired his Chinese workers. After doing so, he ran an ad saying, "I am still before the public and most respectfully solicit a part of your patronage at the Oriental Saloon."[99]

Even though the police court records showed a dreary blank on March 12, 1886, Officer Ben Hyde was busy. About four o'clock in the morning, while Officer Hyde patrolled the back lots of Fourth, Fifth, Allen, and Fremont Streets, he saw a man running from the back of the Crystal Palace Saloon carrying something in his hands. The lateness of the hour and the man's quickened footsteps upon seeing the officer awakened Ben's suspicions, and he ordered the man to halt. Instead of complying, the fellow started to run down Fremont Street. The officer, who fired at him five times, followed closely. Officer Hyde did not know if he shot the man because he escaped in the darkness. In his flight, the fugitive dropped three packages, which the officer recovered. Upon examination, Hyde found the bags filled with coins belonging to parties named Bronk, Morehouse, and Schofield, who were conducting faro games in the Crystal Palace Saloon. The coins, which amounted to approximately four thousand dollars, were taken to the Occidental Hotel for safekeeping, while the saloon's owner, Julius Caesar, was advised of the theft. Upon examining the safe, it was determined the thief knew the combination, because the vault had not been pried open. A key had opened the inner door. Unfortunately, the officer had not recognized the thief and had no leads. Needless to say the combination to the safe was immediately changed.

A few days later, business was back to normal at the Crystal Palace, and the faro dealers were having a streak of luck. It was reported by the newspaper that "it was so cold for some of the faro players last night in the Crystal Palace Saloon, that the frigidity actually frosted the windows adjacent to the game."[100] Billy Hopkins was new to the Crystal Palace and served the "bibulous" for Caesar.

Sometimes miners earned enough money from their toils to open a business. Well-known miner Jack Martin was one of those fortunate souls. When he opened the Arcade Saloon in March, the Tombstone Brass Band performed selections, while the Tombstone Glee Club sang popular songs. Jack, also associated with the State of Maine mine, was married two months later. A few months after that, when election season drew closer, Jack was encouraged by many to run for chief of police.

People who lived in a mining town tended to be more transient than others. They adapted to their surroundings and changed as the town did. "Uncle" Al Richards was a forty-four-year-old man from England who enjoyed many lively businesses in Tombstone. He sold liquors at the Grand Central Saloon until late March 1886, when he closed his business on Allen. On April 2, he opened a new saloon business on Fourth Street and called it the Opera Saloon. His opening that evening included a free lunch, music, and a fine line of wines and spirits. Eight months later, Al opened another new saloon on Allen Street in the building formerly occupied by the Star Restaurant. He requested that everyone attend his opening and enjoy the free turkey lunch.

Ike "Keno Ike" Isaacs purchased the saloon formerly occupied by Charles Mauk. Mauk left Tombstone and retired to a ranch in the

Huachuca Mountains. Isaacs remodeled the saloon and ordered a supply of fine wines, liquors, and cigars. He named his saloon the Delta,
after the old Virginia City saloon with the same name. He invited
everyone to his grand opening at nine o'clock on March 22, 1886. Ike's
keno saloon was well received and, from early morning until late in the
evening, was thronged with visitors. At ten o'clock, an elegant, free
lunch was served. Ike also served Anheuser lager beer on tap. Pat
Holland was his bartender during the day shift. The *Daily Tombstone*
said, "Any person wanting a cool drink of 'analyzer' beer, can procure
the same by calling on Pat Holland on the morning watch at Ike's."[101]
Ike offered a rare display of photographs at his saloon that contained
pictures of every notable sporting man, slugger, wrestler, and foot
racer in the world. Holland added to the photo exhibition, but the
photo was not of a sporting man, but of Geronimo's wife. Since
Tombstone was a sporting town, people bet on just about anything.
Ike Isaacs was no different. He placed a challenge in the local paper
claiming he had an unknown barber who could cut hair fast. He
backed his barber in a challenge against any in town to a haircutting
match. Three months later, Ike sold his business to the oldest saloon
man in town, Jack Doling. Doling had been in Tombstone since its
earliest beginnings and was well versed in serving Tombstone's
favorite drinks.

By the end of March, the Crystal Palace Saloon had discharged all
of its Chinese help, making it the last saloon to do so. With that final
action, none of Tombstone's saloons employed Chinese. The anti-
Chinese movement was still active, and on March 27, the league, which
numbered 485 members, held another meeting. This time no formal
speakers were called upon, but each member was asked to speak
about the movement. It appeared the boycotting of businesses that
employed Chinese was working, but had not eliminated the "problem." League members were again encouraged to boycott those businesses and to find other places with which to do business. Saloon
owner Joseph Mellgren spoke, stating the movement had so far been
a success. He also said he supported this movement because he was
not just looking out for himself, but for his children, who were growing up and would have to "fight this evil."[102]

The Tribolet brothers were prominent businessmen in Tombstone,
especially during its earlier years. When they arrived in Tombstone,
they set up meat markets and also saloons where they brewed their
own beer. They were involved in other ventures, including mining.

Sigfried, who owned the Golden Eagle Brewery, wrote a letter to the paper in March 1886 regarding his older brother's recent actions. Charley Tribolet had been given a government contract to sell meat to Geronimo. However, rumors circulated that Charley sold liquor to Geronimo and his men. To dispel the accusations, Sigfried wrote a letter to the editor of the *Daily Tombstone*. His letter stated the rumors about his brother were preposterous, and Charley was only selling meat to Geronimo. He did, however, describe an incident that occurred in Sonora, Mexico, which may have led to the rumors. According to Sigfried, "When Geronimo and his crowd came to Tribolet's tent they wanted fire water; at that time Mr. Tribolet was alone and had some liquors in the tent which he gave up in order to save his own life and also gave the Indians control of his premises. If any one can say that he sold liquor to the Indians under these circumstances, he is either a knave or a fool...furthermore that the person or persons who sent the blackmailing dispatch to Tucson was some damned drunken liar."[103] The story, the rumors, and the accusations were never settled. By January 1900, Sigfried Tribolet had moved from Tombstone to Phoenix, where he operated Tribolet's Cold Storage Market.

On March 30, 1886, twenty-three-year-old James Hennessey and partner, Charlie Driscoll, who for the past four years owned the Capitol Saloon, relocated to the Can Can's old location under the name of the Criterion saloon. Before their grand opening, they refitted the building and spared no pains or expense.[104] An elegant lunch was spread for the grand opening of this bijou saloon. Even though the owners renamed their saloon, many patrons called it the Capital Saloon. The Criterion sported a new sign; the background was black, and the name was painted in gold script. Hennessey also served on the grand jury committees to inspect the office of the district court, justice courts and constables, and treasurer's office. Shortly after opening their saloon, the men witnessed a scrapping match fought under the Marquis of Queensberry rules. After just two rounds, the match was declared a draw. Because their saloon had fast become a popular resort in town, they added a faro table. Dealer Billy Moore set up a table in the back and claimed nothing but a square game was dealt. When the summer months arrived, the climate proved too much for Jimmy, who was forced to leave Tombstone for Lake Bigler, California. He planned to stay there until the fall and then return home.

Occasionally, some of Tombstone's old pioneer residents stopped back to visit. Gus Lee, who once owned the Criterion saloon, and one of Tombstone's earliest saloonkeepers, had been gone for three years and lived in Nogales. In mid-April, he came to town for a visit with old friends. Gus was one of Tombstone's best banjo players, and his many friends welcomed him home hoping he would serenade them with a banjo solo. After only one day in Tombstone, Lee announced he had decided to stay. He was quickly hired by Frank Broad to serve as mixologist at his saloon. The saloon owner bug bit Lee again, and about a month later, along with Ben Woods, Gus opened a new saloon called the Senate. The Senate was located on Allen, between Fifth and Sixth Streets. Their grand opening was largely attended and patrons enjoyed band music and a hearty lunch spread, which included bread poultice and mock turtle soup.

Gus, whose aliases were "Spots" and "Baldy," later offered silver tailed herrings as part of his free lunch spread. During the summer, Gus initiated a new lunch at the Senate, calling it the IXL pistol lunch. It was also at this time when Gus and his bartender, Ben Woods, introduced Tombstone to their rawhide band for the first time. The two were considered expert banjo players.

Mint juleps, mint toddies, and all kinds of "cooling" drinks were the latest items available at Mellgren's Oriental Saloon in April 1886. William Nichols was the "prince mixologist" at the Oriental who served up house specialties and Anheuser beer on tap. Nichols was well-known in town and was hired by Mellgren shortly after he discharged his Chinese help. Despite this, an odd advertisement appeared in the paper around the same time. "Chalee Melglen, him no good man. Bombi his shaloon closee up. Chinese no patlonize him; him alle same Ilishamn. Alle Chinamen no go to Melglen no more—You shabbe?"[105]

Mellgren sold the Oriental the following month, when Elwood Maden, a former Tombstone resident, returned home. Mellgren took up mining for a while then reopened Tombstone's swimming pool. Maden & Co. quickly refitted the Oriental and hired Charles Rainey as its mixologist. Toward the end of summer, Maden sold the Oriental to John Burns, a former partner in the Elite Restaurant in town.

Tom Walker was putting a new bar in his wine rooms and making other general improvements when he hired "Captain" Myron Converse. Converse served a variety of drinks behind his new bar, but his specialty was champagne flips. A few weeks later, Walker's bar was adorned with two beautiful oleograph pictures he received from San

Mint julep illustration, *Harry Johnson's Bartender's Guide*, 1882, from the author's collection.

Francisco liquor dealers, Stroufe & McCrum. The paintings measured five by three feet and represented scenes of historical interest. As with many who lived in this transient town, Tom had left Tombstone for a new bonanza camp at Stein's Peak by year's end.

Faro games could often turn into trouble, and that's just what happened to saloon owner Andy Meagher. A complaint was filed by Police Officer Coyle against Meagher on the charge that he defrauded William Bradley. The charge claimed he allegedly took $105 from Bradley by means of a "brace" faro game. The charges were eventually dropped.[106] That pleased Meagher on many counts, especially since he had already proclaimed that he "had enough of Tombstone" and was reportedly

Comet Saloon's letterhead, courtesy of the Arizona Historical Society.

heading for Canada.[107] Meagher finally got to leave Tombstone about three months later, and was said to be running a saloon in Silver City, New Mexico.

In late April 1886, dance house owner and miner Pasquale Nigro gained attention when he received a handsome gift from a liquor firm in Chicago. It was said Nigro was given one of the most elegant bar lamps ever seen. A month later, he dug an immense wine cellar next to his saloon and offered a new French line of refreshments, including cognac and wine. Nigro advertised pool and billiard tables were connected with his Comet Saloon. Nigro also kept busy at his Margarita Mine. By the fall, Nigro had closed the business and headed for Bisbee, Arizona.

Ravell, the famous tenor of Mapleson's opera troupe, had recently severed his ties with his troupe and started his solo career at the Crystal Palace Saloon. A few days later, Miss Birdie Woods made her debut at the Crystal Palace. Shortly thereafter, Ben Wehrfritz sold his share of the saloon to his partner, Julius Caesar. On May 8, Ben sold his business to Julius for eight hundred dollars, which included the furniture and liquor stock. Fred Parker, who maintained a chophouse in the saloon, also left. Parker, however, only moved his chophouse to a new location, which was previously occupied by the Cuba Cigar store. His new restaurant, renamed the Elite, was located next door to Driscoll and Hennessey's Criterion Saloon.

About a month and a half later, Julius Caesar left the business, too, selling the entire contents of the Crystal Palace Saloon to William H.

Curnow, a former Tombstone miner, for six hundred dollars. The transaction included barrels of whiskey, gin, sherry, French champagne, cognac, brandy, a piano, and a counter music box. Even though the Caesars sold their business to Curnow, they retained ownership of a storage room in the back of the Crystal Palace for making beer. Caesar, a former restaurant man, set up a lunch counter in the back of the saloon where Parker had his chophouse. On May 16, 1889, Sophie and Julius Caesar leased the ice storeroom in the rear of the Crystal Palace Saloon to Joseph Tracy for fifteen dollars for six months. Caesar's old partner, Bernhardt Wehrfritz, left Tombstone and had a saloon in Nogales, Arizona. Its name? The Crystal Palace!

Saloon drinks aside, soda was a popular refreshment in town. Not only did it complement many of Tombstone's mixed drinks, but it also tasted good alone. On May 5, 1886, the *Daily Tombstone* wrote, "While not wishing to detract from the merits of the summer drinks supplied by the various wet groceries in camp, it is an undeniable fact that the cream soda at Yaple's is a remarkably palatable one." Sarsaparilla, once sold as soda in Tombstone, was back to being sold as medicine. It was said to cure those with sunken eyes and a pallid complexion. Ayer's sarsaparilla was said to be just the cure.

After deciding to close his business in June, Albert Fortlouis, liquor and cigar dealer, assigned his remaining inventory to H. J. Sadler to satisfy his creditors. Shortly after leaving Tombstone, Fortlouis and his wife had a baby boy.

With all the saloons in town, it's no wonder there was a problem with too many beer barrels lying in the streets of Tombstone. The *Daily Tombstone* wrote, "Two or three old drunks volunteered to fight Indians this afternoon if the citizens would supply them with an oyster can and some crackers and cheese. The enemy they were to meet were the numerous beer barrels that are piled up in front of the saloons on Allen Street."[108]

Saloon owner Gilbert Bradshaw started a new Bisbee stage line with partner T. Taft on July 1, 1886. A few months later Bradshaw married Mrs. Frankie Stump. Around the same time, John B. Ayers, of Charleston, bought Bradshaw's Fashion Saloon. Ayers added a billiard table and promised a free lunch at his grand opening. Bradshaw also may have started a new trend in treating wounded horses. A horse at L. W. Blinn's Lumber Mill was found with a broken front leg, and Blinn ordered the horse shot. Upon learning this, Bradshaw requested the horse be given to him. Bradshaw's next stop was Dr. Goodfellow's office, where the horse's leg was set. It immediately stood up and was saved from certain death.

Likely convinced Tombstone's future was secure, despite recent news of the fire in the Grand Central mine's main shaft, Harry Stevenson of the Willows Saloon planted a flower garden in the rear of his saloon. His business was reportedly doing so well that he purchased a new safe and installed a refrigerator to keep his beer cold. Harry's brother, George, who had arrived from San Francisco a month earlier, worked for him at the saloon. Harry was known for displaying various items in his saloon—this time it was a coxcomb. He picked this plant from his garden to display because it had grown in the shape of an ostrich. While Harry's business was doing well, his brother George's health was not. George, who had suffered from rheumatism for some time, decided a visit to San Francisco might make him feel better; he left on July 18.

Just in time to see the fireworks display in Tombstone, Colonel "Fred" Hafford returned to Tombstone after being gone for some time. When Hafford had paid a visit to Tombstone the previous year, he told acquaintances he was on his way to Kingman, Arizona, to set up shop. At that time he applied for a patent to turn the Spanish bayonet plant into fiber, which he would make into sacks. Hafford, along with partners John Belk and William Herring, were finally ready to begin their American Fibre Company. The company proposed to make rope and twine from the Spanish bayonet plant, which grew profusely in the surrounding areas.

Back in town for a little over a month, Colonel Hafford's rope and twine venture went insolvent. He scouted Phoenix for possible prospects, but failed to find anything of interest. Hafford returned from Phoenix and opened a saloon where Stevenson & Crowley's Willows Saloon had once been. Stevenson moved the Willows Saloon one block farther up on Allen where Ashmun & Walker once had their saloon. It was located next door to the Can Can Restaurant and the *Daily Tombstone* newspaper. Stevenson and his partner, Crowley, separated when Crowley purchased the Elite Saloon. In September, Crowley sold the saloon. The purchaser was Tombstone pioneer John Cody. Cody had been gone for six years and was once proprietor of the Mining Exchange saloon. He purchased the Elite Saloon from John Crowley. According to the papers, "Uncle John," as he was familiarly called, was known in Arizona and California for his saloon talents.

As 1886 wound down, founder Ed Schieffelin's Tombstone had changed a great deal since he first witnessed the boom. As Election Day neared, people in the territory became nervous about how people would act. To ensure a little more civility throughout the territory, the Arizona legislature proposed a new bill. Anyone who owned a saloon, drinking palace, or beverage house was not allowed to sell, give away, or furnish spirituous beverages on general election day. The fine for violating this act was fifty to three hundred dollars.

Tombstone's saloons, while their numbers decreased as time went on, managed to endure the closing of the mines and the relocation of the county seat.

Chapter Three

Drunk, Disorderly, and Just Plain Offensive

Tombstone was a city known for many things—mining, drinking, and gambling—just to name some of the more exciting activities. Along with this excitement, and not to mention money, trouble usually followed.

Tombstone saw its share of tramps, vagrants, sham artists, thieves, and cattle rustlers. The town also did a pretty good job dealing with these troublemakers. The law in Tombstone, for the most part, took care of the daily incidents, despite what some in town thought.

A strange event took place on a hot summer evening when thieves broke into Danner & Owens's saloon. Oddly enough, the only thing they took was a large quantity of blankets. The *Epitaph* reported that this incident was the third or fourth crime of its nature to take place. They said, "The town is being worked by a band of petty larcenists." In light of this, the newspaper mocked Tombstone's law officers by remarking that their mining camp was without a "chief." It was customary in most new mining camps to have what was called a "chief." He was a man with brevity and control, who could handle a knife and a pistol. Tombstone needed such a man to step forward for this "position." The newspaper reported no one in Tombstone had done so yet. They were relieved, however, when a reporter strolled by an Allen Street saloon and heard someone declare he was the man for the job. He was overheard saying he was the "Gamest man in seventeen territories, wasn't afraid of as many officers as could stand between two streets, the click of a six-shooter was music to his ears, and the glitter

151

of a knife was like pepper to his soup." Unfortunately, the reporter's hopes were dashed when he saw the town's new "chief," who was an elderly, gray-haired man, being arrested by Officer Bennett. The *Epitaph* said, "'Twas alas, too true, and Tombstone still languishes without a chief."[1]

Tombstone had many colorful characters living within its boundaries, including one individual known as the "Gila Monster." She was a well-known prostitute, and one Sunday fall afternoon in 1880 she filled the air with a string of profane and obscene language. Many people were offended by her remarks, and an *Epitaph* reporter advised someone should see to it this type of thing didn't happen too often.

It should come as no surprise that despite Tombstone's level of sophistication, it wasn't perfect. The streets were dusty, the flies were bad, and crime existed. A miner named Mike "Red Mike" Ryan became involved in a string of unusual and illegal events.

To begin with, Mike had been released from jail in early July after being held six months awaiting trial on an attempted murder charge. Around July 10, 1881, a nineteen-year-old farmer named Douglas Lilly was robbed of a silver watch and a pocketbook containing five dollars. A short time before the robbery, he had had the watch repaired at Seamen's Jewelry store in town. Thinking the thief might try to pawn the watch there, Lilly informed the owner of the store of what had happened. Sure enough, a bootblack named Chromo brought the watch in to the store on July 20. City Marshal Virgil Earp was notified and immediately began questioning Chromo. During the interview process, Chromo said he purchased the watch from "Red Mike" for five dollars. At the time, Mike was serving a fifteen-day sentence for carrying a concealed weapon. If he didn't have a good reason for being in possession of the watch, he would have been given an extended stay. A couple of days later, Mike had paid his fine for carrying a concealed weapon and was again at liberty.

From the time he was released from his six-month stint in jail, and before being arrested for carrying a concealed weapon, Mike got into more trouble. On July 14, he became slightly intoxicated and roamed the streets of Tombstone with a great roll of greenbacks in his hand. Mike offered to bet anyone from five cents to a thousand dollars on the ace "straight up." As the night wore on, Mike became more inebriated and eventually leaned against an adobe wall half asleep. Three "sharks" approached Ryan, and upon seeing this, Marshal Earp brought Ryan into custody. Earp took $230 from Ryan's overalls for safekeeping, put him to bed, and released him in the morning.

After his narrow escape from the sharks, Ryan realized Marshal Earp had not found all his money. Since Ryan had this money burning a hole in his pocket, he decided to "blow it in" in good style. Calling upon everyone he saw in the Golden Eagle Brewery, he invited them "to toss the ruby."[2] As willing participants surrounded him, Mike was "jostled" and the thieves took two one-hundred-dollar bills. The perpetrators clumsily committed their crime and were seen by a dozen or so witnesses who easily identified them. A warrant was sworn out for William Freeman, alias "Red Billy," and his accomplice, Jim Bennet, shortly after they committed the crime. "Red Billy" hired a team of horses with his newfound fortune and set out for Charleston. The deputy sheriff in Charleston received the dispatch too late from Tombstone to catch the crook, and "Red Billy" headed for Benson. Tombstone's city marshal, Virgil Earp, telegraphed his brother, Morgan, who was in Benson at the time. It was again too late; "Red Billy" boarded the train.

Marshal Earp arrested his partner in crime, Jim Bennet, after he tried to get a one-hundred-dollar bill changed at one of the feed corrals. "Red Billy" eventually joined his partner when later that day, "Red Billy" returned to Benson, where Morgan Earp arrested him and returned him to Tombstone. Bennet was later acquitted for lack of evidence, and "Red Billy" skipped town for parts unknown.

The *Daily Nugget* deemed Mike Ryan a "persistent offender" after he became involved in yet another incident.[3] Since the Golden Eagle Brewery previously proved a "hostile" environment for Mike, he chose to take his business to Lou Rickabaugh's Oriental clubrooms. The Oriental proved just as bad for Mike, but this time from his own doing. For reasons unknown, he helped himself to a twenty-dollar piece from one of the faro table draws.

Ryan was promptly arrested and taken to the city jail by Marshal Earp. Earp later brought in a "fellow full of joy" and put him in the cell with Ryan. About an hour later, as Earp took Ryan to the county jail, Ryan suggested he and the marshal stop in for a drink somewhere. Earp replied, "On what? You haven't a cent." "Ain't I though?" said Ryan. "What do you call that?"[4] He showed Earp four bits and a ten-cent piece. When asked where he got the money, Ryan informed the marshal he had rolled his cellmate and found it! Ryan was arraigned and taken before Judge Wallace on July 19, whereupon he pled not guilty and demanded a jury. Mike claimed he did not roll his cellmate and implied Marshal Earp lied.

The fear of snakebites caused some citizens to do strange things. Dan Nichols was known as a remarkably sober and industrious laborer. Yet he found himself standing before a judge explaining why he had been arrested in July 1881. The judge was clearly surprised and quite puzzled when Dan was brought before him. Dan was charged with being drunk and disorderly, to which he pled guilty. He then explained to the judge that he only fell from grace because he had taken some of the "Oh to be joyful" to prevent snakebites. The judge then gave Dan a lecture on the evil of such activities and pointed out that if he continued this "snake bite prevention," it would eventually bring "the snakes" to him.[5] The judge fined Dan five dollars to make an impression he would not soon forget.

Another poisonous creature that frequented Tombstone's homes and businesses was the centipede. Averaging five to six inches in length with sharp pinchers, these creatures were feared. They also caused significant pain to most who were unfortunate enough to be bitten by them. Trying to disprove the theory these insects could not bite, John Young put one of them on his arm and pinched its tail. The centipede angrily responded with a bite to Mr. Young's hand. Young's hand swelled shortly after the bite, and all the known poison antidotes were tried. All were unsuccessful, and Young suffered in great pain. His hand was soaked in ammonia, and he consumed great quantities of whiskey to ease his suffering. It was reported Young was delirious for a day, and it was thought he would not live. He did, however, survive.

It was also in July when a warrant was sworn out for John Henry "Doc" Holliday. His girlfriend, Kate Elder, accused him of attempting to rob the U.S. Mail and killing the stagecoach driver, Eli "Bud" Philpott. Even though the murder and holdup had taken place four months earlier, the warrant wasn't sworn out until now, when Kate signed an affidavit against Doc. Holliday was arrested but was let out on five thousand dollars bail. The men who supplied the bail were Wyatt Earp, John Meagher, and Alhambra Saloon owner, Joseph Mellgren.

The Chinese quarter in Tombstone proved to be one of great despair for many in town. In addition to the laundries, gambling parlors, restaurants, and dry goods shops, the Chinese quarter offered another item for sale—opium. Tombstone's men frequented the opium dens, but what frightened the townspeople were the visits being made by their children and women. Because there was a legislative enactment and a city ordinance against selling opium, the citizens hoped action would be taken. Happily for Tombstone residents, Marshal Earp and his officers took action. One night they raided an opium den and arrested five Chinamen who were enjoying a quiet smoke. Officer Bronk handcuffed two of the men together, and when his back was turned, they made a run for it. Because the den had several rooms, and many nooks and shanties surrounded it, the two almost got away. They were taken before Judge Spicer, fined fifteen dollars each, and warned to cease their visits to opium dens.

Judge Spicer's court docket was quite full on September 28, 1881. It included John Madden, who was arrested for fighting and disturbing the peace. Benjamin Trebelcock was arrested for drunkenness and sleeping on the sidewalk. Alfred Thompson was arrested for fighting and disturbing the peace, as were Sam Brown and William Crayton. Soloman T. Anderson was arrested for carrying a concealed weapon, quarreling, and abuse. Mrs. McDonald was brought in for keeping a house of ill fame, and so was Miss Emma Parker. Both ladies pled not guilty and were held over for trial. Mrs. McDonald, dubbed the "much persecuted lady of ill fame," found only one friendly face among her twelve male jurors.[6] Unable to agree on a unanimous decision, the jury was discharged to give the court, officers, and attorneys an opportunity to go over details. Just what happened to the charges against Miss Parker and Mrs. McDonald is unclear. What is clear though is that Emma Parker was not content to live her life in Tombstone unnoticed. A few days after being brought in on charges of keeping a house of ill fame, Emma got into more trouble. She entered the Occidental Saloon about half past one in the morning and began arguing with bartender and owner Gus Williams. She became so noisy and demonstrative that Officers Bronk and Flynn arrested her. Emma did not go quietly, and her screams aroused everyone in the neighborhood. She was booked for being drunk and disorderly, using vulgar language, and fighting. Gus's saloon did a good business despite Emma. He offered keno every night, and gave away $2.50 with the first pot and $2.50 at nine o'clock every night.

Marshal Virgil Earp, upon doing his duty, headed toward the back of the O.K. Corral to disarm some cowboys. Even though the October 26, 1881, gunfight was between the Earps and Doc Holliday and the Clantons and the McLaurys, it affected the entire town.

Politics, thievery, threats, fights, and carrying concealed weapons are what eventually led to the fight. When the smoke cleared, Frank and Tom McLaury were dead, and Billy Clanton died shortly thereafter. Virgil and Morgan Earp were wounded, while Wyatt Earp and Doc Holliday were arrested; and a lengthy preliminary hearing ensued. Testimony from the hearing indicated that Ike Clanton visited several of Tombstone's saloons the evening before the fight and the following morning. The former restaurateur testified he had been in Thomas Corrigan's saloon on the night before the gunfight where he, Virgil Earp, Doc Holliday, Tom McLaury, John Behan, and another man played a fateful game of poker. The game lasted until daylight, then Virgil went home to go to bed, and Ike cashed in his chips.

About eight o'clock that morning, Ike was seen in the Oriental Saloon by bartender Ned Boyle. After Ned finished his shift, he passed Ike on the street in front of the telegraph office. Ned saw Ike's pistol exposed, and since carrying a weapon in town was against the law, Ned covered Ike's gun with his coat and told Ike to go to bed. Ike insisted he would not go to bed and that as soon as the Earps and Doc Holliday showed themselves on the street, "the ball opened" and they would have a fight. After that, Ike headed towards Kelly's saloon.[7] Ned went to Wyatt Earp's house and advised him of Clanton's threats.

Between nine and ten, while the Earps slept, Ike visited Julius Kelly's Wine House. As Kelly tended bar, he overheard a conversation between Ike Clanton and Joe Stump. Kelly testified they "called for drinks" and discussed Ike's problems from the night before. Kelly asked Ike what kind of trouble he had had the previous night. According to Kelly, Ike said the Earp crowd and Doc Holliday had insulted him the night before, when he was not heeled: that he had now heeled himself and that they had to fight on sight.[8, 9]

With the town hearing rumors that the cowboys were ready to fight with the Earps, the marshal and his assistants had no choice but to go and meet the cowboys face to face. Some thirty bullets flew in less than twenty-five seconds, and a town quickly became divided about who was right and who was wrong. According to the *Nugget*'s account, the Vizina mine's whistle was sounded after the firing ceased.[10] The mines on the hill shut down and the miners were all brought to the surface. Several well armed men from the Contention mine were sent to town on a four-horse carriage when it was learned what had happened.

Tombstone chronicler Clara Brown described the incident:

The inmates of every house in town were greatly startled by the sudden report of firearms, about 3 p.m., discharged with such lightning-like rapidity that it could be compared only to the explosion of a bunch of firecrackers; and the aspect of affairs grew more portentous when, a few moments later, the whistles of the steam hoisting works sounded a shrill alarm. 'The cowboys!' cried some, thinking that a party of those desperadoes were 'taking the town.' 'The Indians,' cried a few of the most excitable. Then, after it was learned that a fight had been engaged in between Marshal Earp, his two brothers, a special deputy (Doc Holliday), and four cowboys . . . speculation as to the cause of the affray ran riot. In the midst of this, when the scene upon the streets was one of intense excitement, the whistle again sounded, and directly well armed citizens appeared from all quarters, prepared for any emergency. This revealed, what was not before *generally* known, the existence of a 'Vigilance Committee,' composed of law abiding citizens, who organized with the determination of upholding right and combating wrong, and who agreed upon a signal of action from the mines. Their services were not needed, however, on this occasion.[11]

A writer for *Harper's New Monthly Magazine* arrived in town in the midst of the hearing. He wrote, "The Grand Jury was now in session, and hearing the evidence in the case. It was rumored that the town party, as the Earps were called, would be able to command sufficient influence to go free of indictment. The country cow-boys, on the other hand, were flocking into town, and on one quiet Sunday in particular things wore an ominous look. It was said that should justice fail to be done, the revengeful, resolute looking men conferring together darkly at the edges of the sidewalk together would attempt to take the matter into their own hands."[12]

According to Judge Spicer, who presided over the hearing, Virgil Earp, as City Marshal, and Morgan and Wyatt Earp and Doc Holliday, whom he called upon for help, went to the site of the fight, near the O.K. Corral, for the purpose of arresting and disarming the Clantons and McLaurys. He did not feel there was enough evidence to support a trial.

Just when Wyatt and Doc thought they were done with legal issues, they were arrested. Doc Holliday, Wyatt Earp, and Johnny Ringo were arrested for carrying concealed weapons in January 1882. The case against Wyatt was dismissed, but Holliday and Ringo each paid thirty dollars in fines. Mattie Webb was also arrested for being drunk and disorderly—again.

With the revenue law in place, Tombstone cracked down on those who didn't comply. Johnny Chenowith, owner of the Grand Hotel Bar and wine parlors, was arrested for violating the revenue law because he sold liquor and manufactured tobacco without a license. Michael Martin and R. Dore, late of the Palace Saloon, were also arrested for selling liquor and manufactured tobacco without a license. They fared better than Chenowith, however, and upon presentation of a license, the case against them was discharged.

Tombstone also became safer when an employee of the Fountain Saloon was finally tracked down and arrested by U.S. Deputy Marshal Blackburn and Sheriff John Behan. Before living in Tombstone, Ed Terril had lived in San Francisco where he had become enamored with a chambermaid named Emma Erickson.[13] Despite being a married man with two children, Ed had abandoned his family because he was set on having Emma. Fred Castle, who employed Emma, also employed Ed as a butler at his San Francisco home, and it was there that Ed had first seen Emma. She was a fair-haired, blue-eyed Scandinavian girl, with whom Ed had fallen hopelessly in love.

Emma, said to have been a respectable young girl, refused the advances of lovesick Ed. He tried to coax her into eloping with him, but she turned him down. Worried about Ed's advances, Emma told her aunt and guardian, Rachel Erickson, about his actions. Emma's Aunt Rachel immediately removed her from employment and took Emma to her house. Ed followed them home, and Aunt Rachel informed him he was not allowed in the house. He left but threatened to return. Emma and her aunt thought they had heard the last of Ed, but about two weeks later, he showed up again. It was a Sunday night, and family and friends were gathered at Aunt Rachel's. They were in the sitting room when Ed entered the house through the front door. Before anyone realized he was in the house, he began firing his pistol, first shooting Emma's aunt and then one of her neighbors. Three of his bullets hit Aunt Rachel, one missed, and the other lodged in the neighbor's leg. After emptying his gun, Terril ran down the hallway and into the street. The local policeman, A. W. Haskell, immediately captured Terril. Ed said he was "nigh crazy" because he could not get to the only woman he ever loved. He stated he wanted to kill the aunt, who was the only thing standing in the way of true love. He also told Officer Haskell he planned on killing himself next. The officer asked Terril how he intended to kill himself when he had no bullets left. Ed claimed he "got confused and forgot about it."[14]

Terril was tried in San Francisco before Judge Ferrel for assault with attempt to kill. Of the twelve jurors, one found Terril to be innocent. It was soon discovered that the juror who found Terril innocent was a close personal friend of the accused. Since Aunt Rachel was not in immediate danger and appeared to be getting better, Ed was released on a five thousand dollar straw bond awaiting a new trial. He immediately skipped town and found his way to Tombstone not long after. While in Tombstone, Terril was employed by Tombstone's chief caterer, Isaac "Little Jakey" Jacobs. He was then employed by Mr. Alderson of the Fountain Saloon, where he tended the lunch stand. Ed was a native of France, and the Fountain's lunch stand became known for its French delicacies. The *Epitaph* stated, "During his residence here [Terril] has borne an excellent character for industry and honesty."[15]

Terril's secret past may have stayed just that, save for Tombstone's U.S. Deputy Marshal Blackburn. While visiting San Francisco in August 1882, Blackburn was shown a photograph of a fugitive wanted for attempted murder. Upon seeing the photo, Blackburn told San Francisco Police Chief Crowley that he knew who the man was. Blackburn was given requisition papers from the governor of California and immediately upon returning to Tombstone, arrested Terril at the Fountain Saloon. Arresting officer Haskell arrived in Tombstone a few days later to escort Mr. Terril back to San Francisco, where he awaited his fate.

Getting a simple hair wash and comb proved difficult for William Crayton on December 12, 1882. Crayton, who worked the cigar store for Marshall Williams in the Oriental Saloon, went to Barron's Barber Shop to get his hair done. After having been serviced, Crayton stayed to chat with another customer. An intoxicated man by the name of Edward Benson came in and took exception to what was said, which was of no concern to him. He walked up to Crayton and made an offensive remark, at which time Crayton told him to get lost, and gave him a shove that sent him to the floor. Benson gathered himself up and, drawing a cocked pistol, aimed at Crayton, who ducked behind a barber's chair. The pistol fired, and the bullet lodged in the chair. As Benson tried to cock the pistol again, Crayton grabbed it from him and knocked him to the floor. Officers finally arrived at the scene and marched Benson off to the city jail. According to diarist George Parsons, this was the second time Benson had done this.[16]

In early March 1883, Mrs. Woodman, alias the "Roadrunner," was arrested for the murder of Billy Kinsman. He was a local man whose parents owned the Virginia Lodging House before it was lost to the '82 fire. The couple lived together for about two years, until Mrs. Woodman claimed she was beaten and kicked out by Kinsman. Add to that broken promises of marriage, unrequited love, fear of desertion, and jealousy—it all ended in murder. It was said Mrs. Woodman had threatened murder before, but she had never followed through with her threats.

About half past nine on the morning of March 6, Woodman and Kinsman were seen talking and laughing at the Oriental Saloon, which Billy was known to frequent. Shortly thereafter, a large crowd surrounding the Oriental heard a pistol shot. Wounded Kinsman came running from the saloon, and pistol-wielding Woodman followed right behind him. As he ran from the saloon toward the American Clothing Store, Woodman fired a second shot. Doctors Goodfellow and Matthews arrived to aid the badly wounded Kinsman, who remained at the American Clothing Store. Believing his wounds to be fatal, the doctors ordered Kinsman to be taken to his parents' house on Toughnut Street. Upon hearing the news, Mrs. Kinsman arrived at the clothing store and became uncontrollable when she saw her son's condition. She got down on her knees, hugged and kissed her twenty-eight-year-old son, and said, "My beautiful boy." He responded with, "Mother, I am going to die." She exclaimed, "No! No!" and ran to Dr. Goodfellow, who gave her no hope.[17] The doctor then advised her to go home and prepare a bed for her son. Billy Kinsman died later that day at 2:30 in the afternoon. On May 12, 1883, Woodman's trial began when court convened at 8:30 in the morning. Arguments having been heard from both sides, the jury retired. One-half-hour later, they returned a verdict of guilty on the count of manslaughter.

Opium continued to be a problem, but Tombstone's law officers made another successful raid on an opium den in early November 1884. Chief of Police Coyle and Officer Galloway arrested Ah Foy, Gim Sing, and Sucie for smoking opium and keeping an opium den. The defendants' attorney immediately summoned the judge, and the judge assigned each perpetrator to one hundred dollars bail.

Former Fairbanks saloonkeeper and Tombstone resident, George Berryman, felt the wrath of a woman named "Cornish Annie" in early November 1886. At about four o'clock on a Sunday evening, special officer Ben Hyde heard cries for help coming from a house on

Fremont Street, just below city hall. He approached the house and burst in through the door; he found Annie in her nightdress in the middle of the room and Berryman in agony on the ground in one corner. Hyde demanded to know the cause of the disturbance, so Berryman said, "She has thrown vitriol in my face."[18] Cornish Annie admitted her guilt without regret. The officer rushed Berryman to Young's drugstore and Dr. Dunn was summoned. The acid was thrown directly in Berryman's face, but it only hit the right side and then ran down his cheek and neck. Upon immediate examination, Dr. Dunn advised Berryman he might lose his right eye. Later that week, his upper eyelid was removed.

Cornish Annie, whose real name was Annie Allen, again admitted her guilt. Officer Hyde promptly arrested her. A couple of hours later, as she sat in a cell, Annie asked the officer if acid had gotten into Berryman's eyes. When Hyde said no, she exclaimed, "Damn it; that was just where I wanted it to go!"[19] The following Tuesday she was taken before recorder John Clum, who, upon hearing her confession, charged her with "assault with intent to do bodily harm."[20] She pled guilty and was remanded to the custody of the sheriff the next day. Later, Annie hired an attorney and changed her plea to not guilty.

Court convened the next day, but because Berryman was in too much pain to give his deposition, it was postponed until later in the week. Annie asked to go back to the house so she could obtain some clothing. When she got there, she "fell into a fit." The November 17, 1885, *Daily Record Epitaph* said, "Dr. Willis was summoned and this frail one was soon able to continue her journey to the courthouse." On February 27, 1886, Annie was tried in court for assault to do bodily harm and was found guilty. She was fined seventy-five dollars, but remained in jail until she could pay it.

Chapter Four

Idling Around Town

Entertainment in Tombstone

When Tombstone first began to take on the look of a town, it started out with just a few saloons and gambling halls. However, once the mining became profitable, other forms of entertainment could be found. To keep men from idling around town, Tombstone offered theater performances, a bowling alley in one of the saloons, horse races, baseball, and more. Residents also purchased Louisiana and Mexican lottery tickets.

Cockfights

One ghastly form of entertainment, while popular with many, was not considered socially acceptable. In addition to faro, roulette, monte, and other saloon games, Tombstonians took to the back streets and other various places to watch and bet on cockfights. Ike Isaacs, a well-known faro dealer, was also noted for his game chicken expertise. He claimed Tombstone had more first-class game chickens than any other place in America, since almost everyone owned one. A grand match was held in Schieffelin Hall during the month of August in 1881. Hopeful participants were encouraged to leave their address with Bob Hatch of Campbell & Hatch's Saloon or at the Belliona parlors.

While some chose not to participate in a Sunday afternoon ritual of church, many of Tombstone's male residents gathered to watch feisty yard birds attack each other in brutal cockfights. Albert Young and William Bobier, who lived two miles out of town, were two men who supplied Tombstone with prizefighting cocks. Young was a sixty-seven-year-old from Kentucky, while Bobier, about fifty, hailed from Sherman, Texas. The birds were descended from prestigious Kentucky stock. The elderly men raised the birds on their farm, in addition to growing vegetables, which they sold in Tombstone's markets.

One particularly hot July Sunday afternoon proved to be fatal, not for the birds however, but for one of their owners. It seems that Young and Bobier had sold one of their birds to a Tombstone businessman. This businessman showed up on Sunday with his new bird and challenged Young and Bobier's bird. While Young refereed the fight, Bobier handled the bird.

It was conceded that Young and Bobier's bird lost by a technicality. After much argument, nothing was resolved. The decision fell to the referee, who declared it a draw; all bets were called off. Bobier was not happy and threatened to kill Young for his decision. As the two men walked home together after the fight, Bobier's temper rose again. He began hurling insults at Young. Bobier again threatened to kill him and began insulting Young's mother, who was now resting in her grave. Bobier switched from words to fists. He punched Young in the ear, which knocked him to the ground. Continuing to verbally assault Young, Bobier picked up a large rock. As Young started to run away, he drew his .22-caliber pistol. While running, Young fired the pistol behind him to scare Bobier, not realizing that he had aimed squarely at the man. Young's shot hit Bobier in the heart, and he died instantly. At the coroner's inquest, Young was exonerated from any wrongdoing, mainly because Bobier was known to be quarrelsome, had been drunk, and had previously threatened to kill Young.

Racing

In addition to saloon gambling and cockfighting, Tombstonians raced horses and dogs. In early September 1881, Brook's "Bulldozer" raced against Earp's blue dog, "Jim." They ran two heats around the track, and Bulldozer was the victor. One of Tombstone's pioneer saloon men, Jack Doling, owned the Tombstone Race Course. Many in Tombstone who watched horse and dog races frequented the racecourse, about one mile from town. Jack, being the sporting man that he was, made a novel wager in late September. A gentleman named Frank Miller bet twenty-five dollars he could haul a man in Sheriff Behan's buggy, which was similar to a one-man racing sulky. He claimed he could race from Dexter's stable on Fourth to the racecourse within twenty-five minutes.

Jack Doling, who was known to bet on just about anything, took the wager, and produced the racing passenger. Miller, along with horse and buggy, drove for the track and reached it in eighteen minutes.

An incident after a horse race in mid-June 1882 proved a little scary for Tombstone. After an exciting four-hundred-yard stretch between George Spangenberg's gray and Hayne's sorrel, the sorrel was the victor. Since there weren't any stalls at the track yet, the racehorses were taken home. It seems the sorrel thought he was still racing, and on the journey home, he went too fast, smashing up the buggy he pulled. Hayne, the horse's owner and *Epitaph's* editor, was forced to continue his journey home on foot. The *Epitaph* noted Doling was close to having the new stalls completed in anticipation of the numerous races scheduled for July 3. Doling also purchased a saloon from Mr. Spruance, who owned several lots on Fremont Street and one on Allen, where he had built the saloon. Doling maintained the saloon, while Isaac "Ike" Isaacs, also known as "Keno Ike," ran his card games in the back. Mr. Bourland also had a compartment in the building for his cigar stand.

Before the Thanksgiving ball in 1882, Doling's Park was thronged with spectators to see the horse races. The owners of competing horses offered a one-hundred-dollar free-for-all purse for a half-mile dash. Durkee entered his horse, Captain, Brophy brought Browney, and Brown raced his Kentuckian. Captain, the favorite, took the purse. The second race was a quarter-mile dash between Captain and Eccleston's horse, Billy. Again the favorite, Captain won.

Doling's racetrack was the site of a footrace between Joe Rathburn and E. B. Lang in 1885. While Rathburn was quick, Lang was the victor. Even though Doling's track had been used for racing and baseball games since 1881, the town was looking at a new one. A site for the new grounds was located about two and one-half miles east of town. If completed, the track would have a driving park, enclosed grounds, a new grandstand, as well as many improvements. The location had water, which could be obtained by wells. It would be designated as the Tombstone Driving Park. Trees would be planted and suitable buildings erected to make the park a favorite destination.

In 1886 some five thousand Tombstone residents awoke to a blustery New Year's Day with wind, rain, and snow—not to mention broken water pipes. Many planned to celebrate New Year's at Doling's track watching the races, but before long, a blanket of white snow covered the course, and the race was postponed until January 10.

Racing was also a way to celebrate the Fourth of July. In July 1886, since the city of Tombstone had no plans to celebrate the Fourth, many of Tombstone's business owners took matters into their own hands. Storeowners draped their buildings with red, white, and blue bunting, while others simply sported Old Glory. Pasquale Nigro, owner of the Comet Saloon, planning for his July Fourth party, erected a platform to provide shade for those wanting to dance outside. Jack Doling offered horse racing at his track and advised anyone who intended to enter a horse in the July 4 or July 5 races to do so before July 1. Despite the happy Fourth of July celebration, times had grown tougher for Tombstone by 1886, and more and more people left town.

Prizefights & Wrestling

Prizefighting had also become popular in town, and two gentlemen placed challenges in the *Daily Nugget*. The first man, Tom Collins, better known as Toughnut, challenged any man of his height and weight in America to fight him. He weighed 150 and 1/2 pounds, and was six feet one-half inch. He said, "Don't bar neither race nor color, even an Irishman, for $1,000 to $3,000. Man and money at all times, on the corner of Fifth and Toughnut."[1] The other fighter, James Cassidy, was just as direct. He challenged any man in Arizona for the lightweight championship of Arizona for $100 to $5,000. The fight was subject to the rules of the American Prize Ring. He said, "I mean business, and can be found at Mike Martin's saloon."[2]

Most fight challenges issued in Tombstone were for any man to step into the ring to beat the challenger, but Robert McDonald, of Bisbee, issued a different challenge. McDonald, the lightweight champion, challenged "Professor" Costello, who was the middleweight champion, to a fist encounter. McDonald bet five hundred dollars Costello could not knock him out in four three-minute rounds under the Marquis of Queensberry rules. He allowed Costello to choose the date and the place of the fight.

The Marquis of Queensberry rules were the regulations under which most fights were held. There were nine rules, and the *Republican* published them as follows:

Rule #1. The fight had to be a fair stand-up boxing match, in a 24-foot ring, or as near that size as practicable. Rule #2. No wrestling or hugging allowed. The rounds to be of three or four minutes' duration, and one minute rest time.

M. Martin's saloon license, courtesy of the Arizona Historical Society.

Rule #3. If either man fall through weakness or otherwise
he must get up unassisted, ten seconds to be allowed him
to do so, the other meanwhile retire to his corner, and
when the fallen man is on his legs the round is to be
resumed and continued until the three minutes have
expired, and if one man fails to come to the scratch in the
ten seconds allowed, it shall be in the power of the referee
to give us his award in favor of the other man. Rule #4.
A man hanging on the rope in a helpless state, with his toes
off the ground, shall be considered down. No seconds or
any other person to be allowed in the ring during the
rounds. Rule #5. Should the contest be stopped by any
unavoidable interference, the referee to name time and
place for finishing the contest as soon as possible, so that
the match must be won or lost, unless the backers of both

men agree to draw their stakes. Rule #6. The gloves to be fair-sized boxing gloves of the best quality, and new. Rule #7. Should a glove burst or come off, it must be replaced to the referee's satisfaction. Rule #8. A man on one knee is considered down, and if struck is entitled to the stakes. Rule #9. No shoes or boots with spikes allowed.[3]

Boxing matches in Tombstone had become quite sophisticated by the fall of 1883. Neil McLeod and James Young, both of Tombstone, met one evening, not to box, but to sign legal papers. The papers were articles drawn up so the men could fight for the Police Gazette Championship. The articles stated the two men were competing for the Police Gazette champion medal of Arizona and must fight according to the Police Gazette's rules. The match was supposed to be held at Schieffelin Hall on September 22 between 7:00 p.m. and 10:00 p.m., but McLeod came down with bilious fever, and the match was postponed. The fight was eventually held in early October, and after four short rounds, Young was taken out, and McLeod took the four-hundred-dollar purse.

Prizefighter Neil McLeod was supposed to step into the ring again to fight for his title in early 1884, but because of a discrepancy in the rules it was postponed. His opponent, Frank White, insisted the fight be held under the London Prizefighter rules, while McLeod wanted to fight under the Marquis of Queensberry rules or the Police Gazette rules. White wanted to fight under the London rules, because he could win the title after just one match. Under the other rules, a fighter had to win three times to keep his title.

Another sporting event scheduled to take place was projected to be one of the city's most exciting events. On February 9, 1884, a Greco-Roman wrestling match between "Professor" Ed Wilson and former newspaperman Richard Rule was held. Wilson, a regular at Tombstone's new gymnasium, and Rule met to discuss the conditions of the match. They agreed the match should be held publicly at Schieffelin Hall; the winner would net $250. Both men began their training; Wilson started his day with several miles of mountain climbing, several hours of club swinging, exercising on the horizontal bars, and other muscle-developing activities. Rule, on the other hand, was said to have awakened early, walked to the Pick-'em Up mine and back, which was halfway to Charleston, and during leisure hours, wrestled with prizefighter Neil McLeod.

Richard Rule, 1887, from the author's collection.

Both men appeared on the night of the match and gave the crowd its money's worth. The large crowd filled the main hall, galleries, and additional seating on stage. Even some of Tombstone's female citizens were seen sitting on the stage. At 8:49 p.m. the men met in the center and shook hands. While both men were said to be in fine physical shape, each had a different physique. Rule was described as symmetrical with a graceful build, while Wilson was said to be of massive strength. In action, the men were different as well, Rule being very quick and active, while Wilson was slower in his motions.

The *Epitaph* wrote, "Suffice it to say Rule displayed a knowledge of the science of Greco-Roman wrestling that was a surprise to all and particularly gratifying to his friends. The first fall was scored by Wilson in twenty-one minutes... his opponent made wary by experience, put himself entirely on the defensive, and by resorting to the devices known to wrestlers, exhausted the time without losing another fall, therefore winning the match, the conditions being that Wilson was to

Edith Rule, 1887, from the author's collection.

throw Rule twice in an hour, or lose. The exhibition was conducted throughout, in a manner to meet approval of the audience, which at the close greeted the victor with much applause." When Rule married Edith Anderson in 1887, the *Epitaph* wrote its hopes: "that the little Rules may not transgress the big Rules. It's a poor Rule that doesn't work both ways."[4]

Peter Schumacher was a former resident of Tombstone and one of its old-time wrestlers. He had left for Los Angeles, but came back to town and issued a challenge. Even though this lightweight wrestler was only 148 pounds, he had broken the collarbone of his last challenger. His challenge, appearing in the November 11, 1885, *Daily Record Epitaph*, stated, "I will wrestle any man in Tombstone Greco-Roman or a mixed match for a reasonable purse. Ed Wilson preferred. The match is to take place at the earliest date possible. My weight is 148 pounds." Ed Wilson was the existing Tombstone champion.

In 1886 while Tombstone citizen W. H. Chambers was in Kansas City, Missouri, on his way to Chicago, he visited the *Western Sport* office to place a challenge. He deposited $25 with W. S. Smyth, editor of *Western Sport*, with a challenge for Tombstone's boxing champ,

Peter Schumacher, to fight either Greek George or Evan Lewis. Chambers stated the fight would be Greco-Roman style for $200 to $250 a side and the entire admission receipts. The match was to take place in Tombstone or Kansas City, within sixty days from signing the articles of agreement.

Variety Shows

While respectable theater performances were held at Schieffelin Hall, a new variety theater was about to open. Billy Hutchinson, the proprietor of the Bird Cage Opera House, had gone to San Francisco to secure the services of talented people to perform in Tombstone. The Bird Cage Opera House was opened in late December 1881 and was dedicated by Hutchinson's Variety troupe who performed a new and original series of plays, songs, and dances.

By early 1883, the Bird Cage Opera House had become a well-known spot throughout the West for entertainment. The *Daily Republican* reported performances at the Bird Cage were far superior to what they had been just two months ago. Many famous acts arrived in Tombstone and played at the Bird Cage, but only men and less-than-respectable women saw them. Billy Hutchinson ran the theater, and the *Republican* stated, "Billy's motto is excelsior, and he leaves no stone unturned to get there."[5] Billy offered his patrons sixteen entertainers at each performance. In late February, the Bird Cage prepared for one of its finest performances yet. The Lingard Troupe arrived back in town when Sandy Bob's stagecoach brought them up from Contention. They arrived on the twenty-third at 7:30 p.m., just one-half hour before showtime. William Lingard arrived in town with a severe cold, but it did not stop the entertainer. He and his entire company went directly to the Bird Cage, where they immediately performed, without rehearsing or eating supper. After having a good meal and getting a good night's rest, the troupe performed *Divorcons* the following evening. The Lingard Troupe played for three nights at the Bird Cage.

The Bird Cage announced it had a new company performing on the twenty-fourth, with four new artists. Guests saw performances by Sadie Carrington, Emma Budworth, Mabel Deverne, and Maud Barnes. In addition to the four new artists, Tombstonians saw acrobats, a singing and dancing team, a comedian, and many other performances. General admission to the Bird Cage was twenty-five cents, and boxed seats were rated depending upon their locations. In July

1883, Billy sold the Bird Cage to San Francisco liquor dealers John Stroufe and Hugh McCrum.

The Bird Cage was not the only variety theater in town in 1883. Competing with the Bird Cage, Ben Wehrfritz's Crystal Palace Theatre in Tombstone adjoined his saloon and hosted many evenings of entertainment. On August 1, an event dubbed "Mulligan's Muddle" by the *Republican* newspaper, took place. It seems one Eugene Edmunds arrived in Tombstone, eventually went to Hafford's, and treated some acquaintances to a couple of drinks. He then went to see the show at the theater. Before the performance, he joined his friend Mr. Levin and Ben Wehrfritz on the theater floor where he drank a half glass of Boca beer. About two hours later, he took a seat in one of the theater boxes. Edmunds testified he saw John Mulligan passing by his theater box several times during the performance. He also testified that a couple of girls came into the box with him and tried to get him to buy drinks for them. He refused. Shortly after the show ended, Edmunds was knocked down on the ground and surrounded by a man and two or three women. At the time, he was carrying $430 in paper money, with which he was supposed to pay Tasker, Pridham, & Macneil for supplies. In addition to Mulligan, Edmunds accused William Lang, William Soule, Mollie "Irish Mollie" Cullman, and former Bird Cage stage performer Kate "Kitty Mountain" Pierce of being the parties who assaulted him. All accused parties were arrested and bound over for a court appearance on five hundred dollars bond each. Another theater patron, W. H. Vincent, supported Edmunds's testimony. Vincent stated that he saw Irish Mollie bring up a chair and strike something—at the time, he did not know it was Edmunds. Upon going upstairs, he saw Edmunds lying on the floor. Mulligan and Kitty Mountain were holding him down, while Irish Mollie went through his pockets. He heard Kitty Mountain say, "Have you got it?" To which Irish Mollie replied, "You bet your sweet life I have."[6]

Mollie "Irish Mollie" Cullman, also known as Mary T. Smith, upon being accused of this crime, vehemently stated it was not she who committed the crime, but another woman. When she was brought before Judge Felter, she accused Nellie Goodinson, wife of the piccolo player in the theater's orchestra band, of being the one who did the deed. According to Mollie's story, she had been working his box, in company with Nellie and others, that night. A full fifteen minutes before the alleged robbery, Nellie showed Mollie a large roll of bills, and whispered, "It's all right; I've got it all."[7] Mollie indicated the difficulty afterward occurred because Nellie demanded Edmunds pay for drinks he ordered. He refused to pay and a wrangle took place between them, during which he struck her on the breast. She retaliated by hitting him over the head with a chair, and a falling Edmunds caught her about the legs. While the two of them struggled, Soule, Lang, and Mulligan came into the box and took hold of Edmunds to get the two apart. After that, Mollie left the party, and Edmunds left shortly thereafter. Upon hearing this testimony, the judge had Nellie Goodinson arrested.

Upon being questioned about the validity of the story, Nellie indignantly denied it and gave her own version of what happened. According to Nellie, she went into Edmunds's box and joined the party with which Edmunds was drinking. She stated, "He seemed to have plenty of money and was spending it very liberally." He asked her to have a glass of beer, but she declined saying she only drank wine. He replied, "I have a wife and six children to support and can't afford to buy wine." She then said to him, "If that is the case, old man, you've no business here; you had better put your money in your pocket and go home." About fifteen minutes after she left the box, she heard a row and saw Edmunds struggling with several parties. She heard him say, "They have robbed me" or "They are trying to rob me."[8] After that, she saw him leave. Nellie claimed there was a conspiracy against her by the parties first arrested, who combined together to clear themselves by convicting her. John Mulligan and Mollie Cullman, though later tried, were found not guilty.

By the end of August, Ben Wehrfritz had leased his theater to "Professor" Al King. King was known in Tombstone for his daring feats on the tightrope. He temporarily closed the theater to make renovations, hire about fifteen "pretty waiter girls" from San Francisco and the East, and make it similar to the Tivoli in San Francisco.

King's Crystal Palace Theatre soon opened. It was filled with men enjoying drinks, fine cigars, and a nightly variety show. The actors and actresses performed while patrons watched the show from their seats or private boxes. On September twenty-first, King threw a party in one of the private boxes and liberally showered his guests with bottles of expensive wine. He obtained the wine from many of the local saloons and advised the owners he would make it all right in the morning. About three o'clock that morning, Al King and his wife boarded a buggy in front of the theater. They were driven to Summit Station and boarded the railroad, on which they headed East. The newspapers claimed Al had failed to pay his many creditors, including the actor, and the saloons where he procured the alcohol for his theater. With Al gone, Ben Wehrfritz eventually resumed his position at the theater once again. Wehrfritz continued to offer nightly variety shows and advertised orchestra music. Since mostly men patronized the theater, he offered a special performance on Friday nights for the women and children. In addition to this busy work schedule, Wehrfritz was a member of Tombstone's Fire Engine Company.

In addition to his recent woes, Wehrfritz had to contend with City Inspector Chapman. Chapman reported to the city council that a wall between the rear of the Crystal Palace Theatre building and the billiard room of Bauer & O'Connor's Cuba Cigar store was unsafe, and asked for something to be done about it.

In mid-January 1886, Tombstone's liveliest theater was once again opened. The well-known Bird Cage Theatre had been closed until performer Joe Bignon and his wife, Minnie, purchased it. After taking over, they attempted to rename it the Elite Theatre, but that name never took—even though they advertised it that way in the papers. To make his Elite Theatre a success, Mr. Bignon secured the services of several variety acts, and maintained a good "stock" company. He also claimed he would offer new faces weekly, dramatic performances, and a regular vaudeville show. Not long after reopening, the theater capitalized on the recent anti-Chinese movement that swept through Tombstone. Taking advantage of the Chinese situation, Bignon offered a nightly play entitled *The Chinese Must Go!!* He placed a burlesque on his boards advertising this new play, and men filled the theater. The play was based on the current situation in Tombstone. The final act ended with a Chinaman being put on a burro, with all his laundry implements, and being ridden out of town. While most enjoyed this version of the play, those who attended the final night's performance were treated to a different ending. The Chinaman was put on the burro with his things, but this time the burro refused to be led off the stage. Despite all efforts he stayed put. The *Daily Tombstone* wrote, "The situation was ludicrous in the extreme. His burroship had evidently joined the Pro-Chinese crowd; so far as he was concerned the almond-eyed disciples of Confucius could stay."[9] The audience was so taken with this that they broke out with laughter and cat-calls resonated throughout the theater.

The Elite Theatre, formerly and often called the Bird Cage, rapidly became *the* theater of the Southwest. Owner and manager Joe Bignon booked new entertaining acts to keep the crowds amused. In addition to acting performances and plays, Bignon brought in circus professionals Mr. and Mrs. Taylor Frusch to perform their trapeze acts. With their Bird Cage performances over, the Frusches set up a tent on a vacant lot on Allen Street, between First and Second, and provided a grand outdoor performance. Bignon continued to secure some of the best entertainment available. The Elite's next performances included Miss Eva St. Claia, who was a dashing serio-comic actress. Little Bessie West was six years old and graced audiences with her songs and dances. Miss Maud Courtney sang pretty melodies, along with Miss Lulu Roze. Charles Keene, assisted by John West, William Hickey, and George Parker, handled the comedy.

The Elite offered a special event in early May when it set up a walking match racetrack around the audience. John McGarvin and John Forseek competed for one hundred dollars in a six-hour match. Both men walked heel to toe; they began walking to the left for one hour, and then reversed for another hour. This process continued until the race was finished, when John Forseek was declared the winner. He walked the first mile in nine minutes and beat McGarvin by one lap.

In addition to the Elite's events, a boxing match was held earlier in the month between George Walker and Tom "French" Simmons. Held at eleven o'clock in the evening, the match lasted only three rounds before Walker knocked out Simmons. No sooner had this match ended, when arrangements for a match between Walker and Dick Harris were underway.

As the Fourth of July drew closer, ranchers and prospectors from surrounding areas came to Tombstone for the holiday. Joe Bignon, manager of the Elite Theatre, bought a large quantity of fireworks, and on July 4 provided a beautiful patriotic display in front of his theater. Before the fireworks, a hot air balloon ascended from the Elite, and that afternoon there was a special grand matinee performance. The paper noted, "It is a noticeable fact that since the wives of a number of citizens have gone to California, that the attendance at the Elite Theatre has increased wonderfully."[10] As summer had begun to make its presence known, many Tombstone residents packed up and headed for the California coast. This mostly female exodus occurred in Tombstone every year, as the ladies escaped the blistering heat. Strangely enough, faro games had been running light in Tombstone.

With the mining industry slowing down, it was evident to many in Tombstone the end was near. Some held on to the hope of a miracle, but others closed up shop and headed for the next boomtown. Joe Bignon claimed he closed the Elite Theatre for about two weeks for renovations. However, while this was done, Bignon opened a theater in the newest silver boomtown of Kingston, New Mexico. Almost five years to the day after it opened, the Elite, also known as the Bird Cage, was no longer in business. Bignon stayed in Kingston until that mining town fizzled out. He then went to Phoenix for a short time, and then in 1890, assembled a new troupe and headed back to Tombstone. He leased the old Crystal Palace Theatre and called his new theater the Elite. This time, the name took and Bignon entertained Tombstone residents for a couple more years.

Baseball

By 1882, baseball, America's favorite pastime, had finally made its way to Tombstone. Tombstone announced they were in the process of getting a team of "nine" together, and some were already practicing at Mr. Light's lot on the corner of Third and Safford Streets. Plans had also been made to have a match game between Tombstone's team and the San Pedro nines.

Before the Thanksgiving ball in 1882, Tucson's baseball team arrived to challenge the Tombstone nine in front of a large, excited crowd. The home team's hopes were dashed when they realized Tucson's pitcher was a professional player in the California league. His curve ball was said to look like a black snake going through a wheat field. The match was played with enthusiasm and much betting. To the surprise and dismay of many, the umpire called off all bets because of Tucson's professional pitcher. From the first inning, it was clear Tombstone would not win; the final score was twenty-six to sixteen in favor of Tucson. No hard feelings were held, and the home team invited the Tucsonites back to the Cochise Club for some rest and relaxation. About seven o'clock that evening, the Tucson players dined at Jakey's Grand Restaurant, where they enjoyed fresh fish from Guaymas, oysters from the East, and game from the mountains.

Tombstone's male residents enjoyed many sporting events in town, but one sporting event even attracted the ladies. It was the nation's favorite pastime—baseball. Tombstone's team, called the Picked Nine, was finally formed, and they wore white uniforms with red stockings. Many ladies were present, including Mrs. L. W. Blinn, Mrs. Fowler, and Mrs. Colonel Herring along with her four daughters. It was in early July when they had a game against the Grand Centrals. The game began at 9:20 a.m. and lasted for two hours and forty minutes. The Tombstone nine, struggling at first, made a strong showing in the last two innings;

however, they fell short by four points. The Grand Centrals, in their "sans souci" go-as-you-please style uniforms, beat the Picked Nine by a score of twenty to seventeen.

Shooting

Since guns and shooting were so popular in Tombstone, the Tombstone Shooting Club agreed to match six of its members against any six men in the territory, in any sum from fifty to five hundred dollars to shoot with pistol, rifle, and shotgun. In the latter case, they offered to shoot at pigeons or glass balls, and in the former, snapshooting at glass balls or wheel and fire. They demanded to know who wanted the game.

Swimming

July 4, 1886, was a big day for former saloonkeeper Joseph "Charley" Mellgren and for Tombstone as well. Charley reopened Tombstone's swimming pool just in time to celebrate the nation's holiday. Plans for the reopening had elicited growing excitement. In addition to offering new bathing suits, Charley opened a first-class bar at the bathhouse where he offered the same fine selections he used to offer at his saloon. Before opening the swimming pool, he had refitted the bathhouse and purchased the new bathing suits, which arrived from California. The suits were said to be the finest ever seen in that part of the country. Charley advertised he would have swimming and diving contests with prizes for the winners. Charley made Wednesday and Saturday, from eight to five o'clock, ladies' days. With fifty thousand gallons of water constantly running in and out of the pool, everyone was assured a refreshing swim. Charley also provided a "bus" to and from the pool for the nominal fee of ten cents per ride. Admission to the baths was twenty-five cents, which included a bathing suit and towel. To add to Charley's excitement, his wife presented him with their fourth child, a healthy baby boy, on July 1.

The End

Tombstone and its residents had seen many ups and downs during its brief but exciting heyday. One thing it never lacked was entertainment. Different forms of entertainment slowly began to dwindle as the mines closed and fewer people visited, or called Tombstone home. By the early 1900s, Tombstone's once bountiful population was less than 1,000.

Chapter One

1. Ed Schieffelin, *Destination Tombstone* (Mesa, AZ: Royal Spectrum Publishing, 1996), 77–91.
2. Ibid.
3. Tombstone Mill & Mining Company report, October 26, 1879.
4. Ed Schieffelin, *Destination Tombstone.*
5. Ibid.
6. Ibid.
7. Vosburg's personal account, Arizona Historical Society, September 27, 1925. Arizona Historical Society, Tucson.
8. Ibid.
9. Ibid.
10. *Arizona Citizen*, May 17, 1879.
11. William Miller to Arizona Historical Society, April 11, 1936. Arizona Historical Society, Tucson.
12. Meaning "soiled doves," a euphemism for prostitutes.
13. Porphyry is rock consisting of a compact base.
14. A windlass is an apparatus operated by hand or machine for hoisting. It consists of a drum or cylinder upon which is wound a rope, cable, or chain, which is attached to the object being lifted—usually a bucket.
15. A kibble or "whim bucket" is a mining term that refers to a bucket made of wood and bound with iron. It was used for raising quartz to the surface, bailing, lowering timber, and other purposes.
16. Tombstone Milling & Mining Company report, October 26, 1879.
17. Ibid.
18. William Miller to Arizona Historical Society, April 12, 1936. Arizona Historical Society, Tucson.

19. *Arizona Daily Star*, January 17, 1880.
20. *Arizona Quarterly Illustrated*, July 1880.
21. Ibid.
22. *Arizona Daily Star*, July 18, 1880.
23. *Arizona Quarterly Illustrated*, July 1880.
24. *Daily Epitaph*, July 27, 1880.
25. *Daily Epitaph*, July 28, 1880.
26. *Daily Epitaph*, July 29, 1880.
27. *Daily Epitaph*, August 13, 1880.
28. Letter from the Witherill collection, Arizona Department Library Archives, Phoenix.
29. Reverend William H. Hill, *Spirit of Missions*, October 1880, XLV, Second Letter to Bishop Spaulding about Arizona, Library of Congress, Washington, D.C.
30. *Arizona Quarterly Illustrated*, October 1880.
31. Lynn R. Bailey, *Tombstone from a Woman's Point of View* (Tucson: Westernlore Press, 1998), 24.
32. *Arizona Quarterly Illustrated*, January 1881.
33. *Mining & Scientific Press*, February 5, 1881, XLII, 88.
34. Ibid.
35. William P. Blake, *The Geology of the Way-Up Mining Claim* (New Haven: Tuttle, Morehouse & Taylor, 1881), 10.
36. *Daily Nugget*, August 3, 1881.
37. Ibid.
38. *McKenney's Business Directory* (Oakland: Pacific Press, n.d.).
39. A stope is an area where ore has been removed around a mineshaft. A winze is an inclined passage from one level to another in a mine.
40. *Daily Nugget*, August 6, 1881.
41. *Daily Nugget*, July 9, 1881.
42. A quartz team was a team of horses who carried the quartz/ore in wagons.
43. *Daily Nugget*, October 4, 1881.
44. *Daily Nugget*, October 19, 1881.
45. *Harper's New Monthly Magazine*, Harper & Brothers, December, 1882 to May, 1883, Vol. LXVI, 493–500.
46. Bailey, *Tombstone from a Woman's Point of View*, 45.
47. *Daily Nugget*, December 2, 1881.
48. *Daily Epitaph*, December 7, 1881.
49. *Weekly Epitaph*, December 19, 1881.

50. *Weekly Epitaph*, December 22, 1881.
51. Bailey, *Tombstone from a Woman's Point of View*, 48.
52. According to Tombstone resident Clara Brown, Morgan and Wyatt attended the performance together. Earl Chafin, ed., *Tombstone Letters of Clara Brown* (Riverside, CA: Earl Chafin Press, 1988), 46.
53. Forrestine Hooker, *An Arizona Vendetta*, ed. Earl Chafin (Riverside, CA: Earl Chafin Press, 1998), 33–37.
54. Ibid.
55. *Tombstone Epitaph*, March 20, 1882.
56. Chafin, *Tombstone Letters of Clara Brown*, 47.
57. *Tombstone Epitaph*, November 4, 1882.
58. Bailey, *Tombstone from a Woman's Point of View*, 73.
59. *Republican*, February 23, 1883.
60. *Republican*, July 21, 1883.
61. *Republican*, September 22, 1883.
62. *Republican*, December 29, 1883.
63. *Republican*, January 19, 1884.
64. Patrick Hamilton, *The Resources of Arizona* (San Francisco: A. L. Bancroft & Co., 1884), 154–245.
65. Ibid.
66. Ibid.
67. George W. Parsons, *The Private Journal of George Whitwell Parsons*, ed. Carl Chafin (Tombstone, AZ: Cochise Classics, 1997), 243.
68. *Daily Record Epitaph*, September 2, 1885.
69. *Daily Record Epitaph*, August 19, 1885.
70. *Daily Record Epitaph*, November 1, 1885.
71. Ibid.
72. F. L. Hess, *Glossary of Mining Terms* (U. S. Bureau of Mines, 1885).
73. *Daily Tombstone*, March 12, 1886.
74. *Daily Tombstone*, March 24, 1886.
75. *Daily Tombstone*, March 31, 1886.
76. *Phoenix Herald*, May 3, 1886.
77. Meaning brothel or house of joy.
78. *Daily Tombstone*, May 26, 1886.

Chapter Two

1. *Disturnell's Arizona Gazetteer*, 1881, Bancroft Library, University of California.

2. *Arizona Daily Star*, January 17, 1880.
3. *Daily Epitaph*, September 13, 1880.
4. A disorderly house was another term for house of ill fame.
5. *Arizona Daily Star*, June 20, 1880; actual census shows 2,114.
6. Mrs. Hempe to Arizona Historical Society, recollection letter. Arizona Historical Society, Tucson.
7. Earl Chafin, ed., *Tombstone Letters of Clara Brown* (Riverside, CA: Earl Chafin Press, 1988), 1–3.
8. *Daily Epitaph*, July 22, 1880.
9. *Daily Epitaph*, July 20, 1880.
10. *Daily Nugget*, October 25, 1881.
11. This list appeared in Tombstone's newspaper, the *Daily Nugget*, on August 10, 1881.
12. Dance house was a term often used for houses of ill fame.
13. A demi-monde or demi-monder was someone with a questionable reputation.
14. Lynn R. Bailey, *Tombstone from a Woman's Point of View* (Tucson: Westernlore Press, 1998), 22.
15. *Daily Epitaph*, September 4, 1880.
16. *Daily Tombstone*, July 23, 1880. All of the material quoted here was taken from this article.
17. Estate papers of Otto Esch, Arizona Department Library and Archives, Phoenix.
18. Ibid.
19. *Daily Epitaph*, September 14, 1880.
20. Ibid.
21. These two shots, taken while Holliday was undoubtedly intoxicated, show what a marksman he must have been.
22. *Arizona Quarterly Illustrated*, July 1880.
23. *Tombstone Epitaph*, June 9, 1881. See ad on page 86.
24. Ibid.
25. *Daily Nugget*, July 10, 1881.
26. *Tombstone Epitaph*, June 23, 1881.
27. *Tombstone Epitaph*, June 26, 1881.
28. His severe swelling, which is not typical, may have been caused by an allergic reaction.
29. *Arizona Daily Star*, July 28, 1881.
30. *Daily Nugget*, August 4, 1881.
31. *Daily Nugget*, July 13, 1881.
32. A schooner is a large glass to hold beer; usually a pint.

33. The printer's devil set the type for the newspaper.
34. Clara S. Brown, *Californian*, July 1881, 55.
35. *Daily Nugget*, July 22, 1881.
36. *Daily Nugget*, July 31, 1881.
37. *Daily Nugget*, August 3, 1881.
38. *Daily Nugget*, August 5, 1881.
39. *Daily Nugget*, August 4, 1881.
40. *Daily Nugget*, August 21, 1881.
41. *Daily Nugget*, September 9, 1881.
42. *Daily Nugget*, October 15, 1881.
43. *Epitaph*, October 22, 1881.
44. *Daily Nugget*, October 14, 1881.
45. *Daily Nugget*, October 16, 1881.
46. "Tiger" referred to the faro dealer.
47. *Daily Nugget*, November 4, 1881.
48. Ibid.
49. *Daily Nugget*, November 27, 1881.
50. *Daily Epitaph*, November 6, 1881.
51. *Daily Nugget*, November 6, 1881.
52. *Daily Nugget*, November 16, 1881.
53. *Daily Nugget*, November 17, 1881.
54. *Daily Epitaph*, January 11, 1882.
55. Ibid.
56. *Daily Epitaph*, January 19, 1882.
57. *Weekly Epitaph*, February 13, 1882.
58. *Daily Epitaph*, March 10, 1882.
59. The phrase "barrio libre" means red light district.
60. *Weekly Epitaph*, April 3, 1882.
61. *Daily Epitaph*, January 13, 1882.
62. *Daily Nugget*, May 2, 1882.
63. *Weekly Epitaph*, April 24, 1882.
64. Ibid.
65. *Daily Nugget*, May 2, 1882.
66. Tombstone businesses often compared themselves in stature to California businesses. Many also had connections there or had recently arrived from there.
67. *Daily Epitaph*, May 27, 1882.
68. *Weekly Epitaph*, July 8, 1882.
69. Ibid.
70. *Weekly Epitaph*, July 27, 1882.

71. "Billy the Kid" became a popular moniker after William Bonney made it infamous.
72. George W. Parsons, *The Private Journal of George Whitwell Parsons*, ed. Carl Chafin (Tombstone, AZ: Cochise Classics, 1997), 69. All quotes in this story are taken from this source.
73. *Weekly Epitaph*, December 2, 1882.
74. *Weekly Epitaph*, December 9, 1882.
75. *Republican*, February 23, 1883.
76. *Republican*, July 7, 1883.
77. *Republican*, September 8, 1883.
78. *Republican*, February 9, 1884.
79. Letter from Cuddy appearing in the *Daily Tombstone*, June 18, 1886.
80. John C. Hancock to Arizona Historical Society, recollection letter from Tombstone resident John C. Hancock; the original letter is undated, but was transcribed by the Arizona Historical Society on March 29, 1932, Tucson.
81. John M. "Napa Nick" Nichols.
82. *Daily Record Epitaph*, August 18, 1885.
83. *Daily Record Epitaph*, August 23, 1885.
84. *Daily Record Epitaph*, September 5, 1885.
85. *Daily Record Epitaph*, September 15, 1885.
86. *Daily Tombstone*, January 1, 1886.
87. Ibid.
88. Ibid. All the quotes above are taken from this source.
89. *Daily Tombstone*, January 4, 1886.
90. *Daily Tombstone*, January 16, 1886.
91. *Daily Tombstone*, January 2, 1886.
92. Ibid.
93. *Daily Tombstone*, January 2, 1886.
94. *Daily Tombstone*, March 29, 1886.
95. *Daily Tombstone*, January 16, 1886.
96. *Daily Tombstone*, August 3, 1886.
97. *Daily Tombstone*, March 1, 1886.
98. Ibid.
99. *Daily Tombstone*, March 3, 1886.
100. *Daily Tombstone*, March 18, 1886.
101. *Daily Tombstone*, March 22, 1886.
102. *Daily Tombstone*, March 29, 1886.
103. *Daily Tombstone*, March 30, 1886.
104. *Daily Tombstone*, March 24, 1886.

105.   *Daily Tombstone,* April 15, 1886.
106.   *Daily Tombstone,* April 30, 1886.
107.   *Daily Tombstone,* March 11, 1886.
108.   *Daily Tombstone,* May 19, 1886.

Chapter Three

1.   *Daily Epitaph,* July 22, 1880.
2.   Referring to the dice.
3.   *Daily Nugget,* July 21, 1881.
4.   *Daily Nugget,* July 17, 1881.
5.   *Daily Nugget,* July 24, 1881.
6.   *Daily Nugget,* September 30, 1881.
7.   E. F. (Ned) Boyle's testimony, *Daily Nugget,* November 24, 1881.
8.   "Heeled," meaning he was carrying a gun.
9.   Julius Kelly's testimony, *Daily Nugget,* November 24, 1881.
10.   Reprinted in the *Tucson Weekly Citizen* on October 30, 1881.
11.   *Tombstone Letters of Clara Brown,* Earl Chafin, ed. (Riverside, CA: Earl Chafin Press, 1988), 41–45.
12.   *Harper's New Monthly Magazine,* March 1883.
13.   Author's note: The name was also spelled Terrell.
14.   *Weekly Epitaph,* August 19, 1882.
15.   *Weekly Epitaph,* August 12, 1882.
16.   The first incident happened November 13, 1880.
17.   *Republican,* March 10, 1883.
18.   *Daily Record Epitaph,* November 10, 1885.
19.   Ibid.
20.   Clum returned to Tombstone in 1885–86.

Chapter Four

1.   *Daily Nugget,* October 7, 1881.
2.   Ibid.
3.   *Daily Republican,* July 14, 1883.
4.   *Tombstone Prospector,* October 15, 1887.
5.   *Daily Republican,* February 24, 1883.
6.   *Daily Republican,* August 4, 1883.
7.   Ibid.
8.   Ibid.
9.   *Daily Tombstone,* March 9, 1886.
10.   *Daily Tombstone,* July 1, 1886.

Index